Unlock

Bootstrap 5

Build Modern, Responsive Websites with Ease

A Comprehensive Guide for Beginners and Professionals

Toby Webber

COPYRIGHT NOTICE

DISCLAIMER

The information provided in this book is intended for educational and informational purposes only. While every effort has been made to ensure the accuracy and completeness of the content, the author and publisher make no representations or warranties of any kind, express or implied, about the completeness, accuracy, reliability, suitability, or availability with respect to the book or the information, products, services, or related graphics contained in the book for any purpose. Any reliance you place on such information is therefore strictly at your own risk.

The author and publisher shall not be liable for any loss or damage including without limitation, indirect or consequential loss or damage, or any loss or damage whatsoever arising from loss of data or profits arising out of, or in connection with, the use of this book.

This book may contain links to external websites that are not provided or maintained by the author or publisher. The author and publisher do not have any control over the nature, content, and availability of those sites. The inclusion of any links does not necessarily imply a recommendation or endorse the views expressed within them.

Every effort is made to keep the book up-to-date and running smoothly. However, the author and publisher take no responsibility for, and will not be liable for, the book being temporarily unavailable due to technical issues beyond our control.

The code examples provided in this book are intended for illustrative purposes only. The author and publisher shall not be liable for any errors, omissions, or damages arising from the use of these code examples. It is the responsibility of the reader to adapt and implement the code according to their specific needs and environment.

This book is not affiliated with or endorsed by the Bootstrap team or any other organization. Bootstrap is a registered trademark of Twitter, Inc.

The reader is encouraged to use their own judgment and discretion when implementing the techniques and information provided in this book. The author and publisher shall not be liable for any decisions or actions taken by the reader based on the information contained in this book.

This disclaimer is subject to change without notice.

TABLE OF CONTENTS

Part I: Foundations

CHAPTER 1: INTRODUCTION TO BOOTSTRAP 5

1.1 What is Bootstrap 5?

Alright, let's get this show on the road! If you're reading this, you're probably curious about Bootstrap 5 and how it can help you build awesome websites. Well, you've come to the right place.

In a nutshell, Bootstrap 5 is like a supercharged toolkit for front-end developers. It's a **free**, **open-source CSS framework** that provides a robust collection of pre-designed components, utilities, and JavaScript plugins. Think of it as a set of building blocks that you can use to assemble your website's layout, style its elements, and add interactive functionality.

Instead of writing all the CSS and JavaScript from scratch, Bootstrap gives you a head start with ready-made components like:

- **Grid system**: Easily create responsive layouts that adapt to different screen sizes (we'll dive deep into this in Chapter 2).
- **Navigation bars**: Build sleek and functional navigation menus for your website.
- **Buttons**: Style buttons with various colors, sizes, and states.
- **Forms**: Create user-friendly forms with input fields, labels, and validation.
- **Modals**: Display pop-up windows for important information or actions.
- **And much more!** (We'll explore these components in detail in Chapter 3.)

But Bootstrap 5 is more than just a collection of components. It also provides:

A consistent design language: Bootstrap ensures your website has a cohesive look and feel, making it visually appealing and user-friendly.

Responsive design out of the box: Bootstrap's components are designed to adapt seamlessly to different screen sizes, from mobile phones to large desktops.

Accessibility features: Bootstrap incorporates accessibility best practices, making your website usable by people with disabilities.

Easy customization: You can customize Bootstrap's styles to match your brand or project requirements.

In essence, Bootstrap 5 empowers you to build modern, responsive, and visually appealing websites with ease and efficiency. Whether you're a seasoned developer or just starting your coding journey, Bootstrap can be a valuable asset in your toolkit.

In the next section, we'll explore why Bootstrap 5 is such a popular choice for web developers and the key benefits it offers. Let's move on!

1.2 Why Use Bootstrap 5? (Benefits and Features)

Okay, so we've established that Bootstrap 5 is this awesome front-end toolkit. But you might be wondering, "Why should I use it? What's in it for me?"

Well, let me tell you, Bootstrap 5 brings a whole lot to the table. It's not just hype; it's a real game-changer for web developers of all levels. Here's why:

1. **Speed and Efficiency**

Imagine building a house. Would you rather start by chopping down trees and making your own bricks, or would you prefer to have pre-fabricated walls, windows, and doors ready to go? Bootstrap 5 is like having those pre-fabricated components for your website.

With its ready-made components and utilities, Bootstrap saves you a ton of time and effort. You don't have to write every line of CSS from scratch. Instead, you can focus on the unique aspects of your design and functionality. This means you can build websites faster, meet deadlines more easily, and maybe even get home a little earlier!

2. Responsiveness Made Easy

Remember the days when you had to create separate websites for desktops and mobile devices? Thankfully, those days are long gone!

Bootstrap 5 is built with a mobile-first approach. This means your websites will look fantastic and function smoothly on all devices, from tiny smartphones to massive widescreen monitors. Bootstrap's grid system and responsive utilities make it a breeze to create layouts that adapt seamlessly to any screen size.

3. Consistency and Cohesion

Have you ever visited a website where the buttons looked different on every page, or the navigation menu was completely out of place? It's not a good look, is it?

Bootstrap 5 provides a consistent design language that ensures all your website's elements look and behave harmoniously. This creates a professional and user-friendly experience for your visitors.

4. Accessibility for All

Building websites that are accessible to everyone, including people with disabilities, is not just good practice—it's essential.

Bootstrap 5 incorporates accessibility features and best practices right out of the box. This means your websites will be more usable by people who rely on assistive technologies like screen readers.

5. Easy Customization

Worried that your website will look like every other Bootstrap site out there? Don't be!

Bootstrap 5 is highly customizable. You can easily override default styles, create your own themes with Sass, and tailor the framework to match your brand or project requirements.

6. A Thriving Community and Ecosystem

Bootstrap has a massive and active community of developers. This means you'll find tons of resources, tutorials, and support online. There are also countless third-party themes, extensions, and tools available to enhance your Bootstrap projects.

7. It's Free and Open-Source!

Did I mention that Bootstrap 5 is completely free to use? That's right, no licensing fees, no hidden costs. It's an open-source project, which means you can even contribute to its development if you're feeling adventurous.

So, there you have it! With its speed, responsiveness, consistency, accessibility, customizability, and thriving community, Bootstrap 5 is a powerful ally for any web developer. It's no wonder it's become the world's most popular front-end framework.

In the next section, we'll roll up our sleeves and get our hands dirty by setting up our development environment. Let's get started!

1.3 Setting Up Your Development Environment

Alright, enough talk! It's time to get our hands dirty and set up our development environment so we can start building awesome websites with Bootstrap 5. Don't worry, it's not as intimidating as it sounds.

Here's what we'll need:

1. A Code Editor: This is where you'll write your HTML, CSS, and JavaScript code. There are tons of great code editors out there, both free and paid. Here are a few popular choices:

- **VS Code:** (My personal favorite) It's free, powerful, and has a huge community with tons of extensions.
- **Sublime Text:** A fast and lightweight editor with a clean interface.
- **Atom:** Another free and open-source editor developed by GitHub.
- **Notepad++:** A simple and reliable option for Windows users.

2. A Web Browser: You'll need a web browser to view your website as you build it. Chrome, Firefox, Safari, and Edge are all good options.

3. Bootstrap 5 Files: You can download the Bootstrap 5 files from the official website (getbootstrap.com). You'll find compiled CSS and JavaScript files, as well as the source code if you want to customize the framework.

Now, let's set up a basic project:

1. Create a Project Folder: On your computer, create a new folder for your project. Give it a descriptive name, like "my-bootstrap-project."

2. Download Bootstrap 5: Go to the official Bootstrap website and download the compiled CSS and JavaScript files. You can choose to download the entire package or just the individual files you need.

3. Create an HTML File: Inside your project folder, create a new file named `index.html`. This will be the main file for your website.

4. Link Bootstrap 5: Open your `index.html` file in your code editor and add the following code within the `<head>` section to link the Bootstrap CSS file:

```
<!DOCTYPE html>
<html lang="en">
<head>
    <meta charset="UTF-8">
    <meta name="viewport" content="width=device-width,
initial-scale=1.0">
    <title>My Bootstrap Project</title>
    <link rel="stylesheet" href="css/bootstrap.min.css">
</head>
<body>

    <script src="js/bootstrap.bundle.min.js"></script>
</body>
</html>
```

Make sure the paths to the CSS and JavaScript files are correct relative to your project folder.

Pro Tip: Consider using a Content Delivery Network (CDN) to link Bootstrap files. This can improve your website's loading speed. Here's how you can link Bootstrap 5 from a CDN:

```
<link
href="https://cdn.jsdelivr.net/npm/bootstrap@5.3.0/dist/css/
bootstrap.min.css"    rel="stylesheet"    integrity="sha384-
9ndCyUaIbzAi2FUVXJi0CjmCapSmO7SnpJef0486qhLnuZ2cdeRhO02iuK6F
UUVM" crossorigin="anonymous">
```

That's it! You've now set up your basic development environment for Bootstrap 5. You're ready to start writing code and building your first web page.

In the next section, we'll do a quick review of HTML and CSS for those who need a refresher. If you're already comfortable with these languages, feel free to skip ahead to Section 1.5, where we'll build our first Bootstrap project.

1.4 Basic HTML and CSS Review (for Beginners)

Okay, before we dive headfirst into Bootstrap 5, let's take a quick detour and review the fundamentals of HTML and CSS. If you're already a web development pro, feel free to skip ahead to the next section. But if you're new to this whole coding thing, or just need a little refresher, stick around!

Think of HTML as the skeleton of your web page. It provides the structure and content, defining things like headings, paragraphs, images, and links. CSS, on the other hand, is like the skin and clothes. It styles the HTML elements, controlling their appearance with colors, fonts, spacing, and layout.

HTML: The Building Blocks

Here's a quick rundown of some essential HTML elements:

- <h1> to <h6>: Headings, with <h1> being the largest and <h6> the smallest.
- <p>: Paragraphs of text.
- <a>: Links to other web pages or resources.

- <img>: Images.
- <div>: A generic container for grouping other elements.
- <ul> and <li>: Unordered lists (bullet points).
- <ol> and <li>: Ordered lists (numbered lists).

Here's a simple example of an HTML document:

```
<!DOCTYPE html>
<html lang="en">
<head>
    <meta charset="UTF-8">
    <title>My First Web Page</title>
</head>
<body>

    <h1>Welcome to My Website!</h1>
    <p>This is a paragraph of text.</p>

    <a href="https://www.example.com">Visit Example
Website</a>

    <img src="images/my-image.jpg" alt="My Image">

</body>
</html>
```

CSS: Adding Style and Flair

Now, let's add some style with CSS. There are three main ways to apply CSS to your HTML:

1. Inline Styles: Add CSS directly to an HTML element using the style attribute.

```
<p style="color: blue; font-size: 16px;">This is a blue
paragraph.</p>
```

2. Internal Stylesheet: Add CSS within the <head> section of your HTML document using the <style> tag.

```
<head>
    <style>
        p {
            color: green;
            font-family: sans-serif;
        }
    </style>
</head>
```

3. External Stylesheet: Create a separate CSS file (e.g., styles.css) and link it to your HTML document using the <link> tag.

```
<head>
    <link rel="stylesheet" href="styles.css">
</head>
```

Here's an example of a CSS rule that styles all paragraphs:

```
.p {
  color: red;
  font-size: 18px;
  line-height: 1.5;
}
```

This rule selects all <p> elements and sets their text color to red, font size to 18 pixels, and line height to 1.5.

CSS Selectors: Targeting Specific Elements

CSS selectors allow you to target specific HTML elements for styling. Here are a few common selectors:

- Element Selector: Selects all elements of a specific type (e.g., p, h1, div).
- Class Selector: Selects elements with a specific class attribute (e.g., .highlight).
- ID Selector: Selects a single element with a specific ID attribute (e.g., #my-paragraph).

CSS Properties: Controlling Appearance

CSS properties control various aspects of an element's appearance. Here are a few examples:

- color: Text color.
- font-size: Font size.
- font-family: Font family.
- background-color: Background color.
- margin: Space outside the element.
- padding: Space inside the element.

Putting It All Together

Here's an example that combines HTML and CSS to create a styled web page:

```
<!DOCTYPE html>
<html lang="en">
<head>
    <meta charset="UTF-8">
    <title>My Styled Web Page</title>
    <style>
        h1 {
            color: blue;
            text-align: center;
        }
        p {
            color: green;
            font-size: 16px;
        }
    </style>
</head>
<body>
    <h1>Welcome to My Website!</h1>
    <p>This is a styled paragraph.</p>
</body>
</html>
```

This code creates a web page with a blue heading centered on the page and a green paragraph with a font size of 16 pixels.

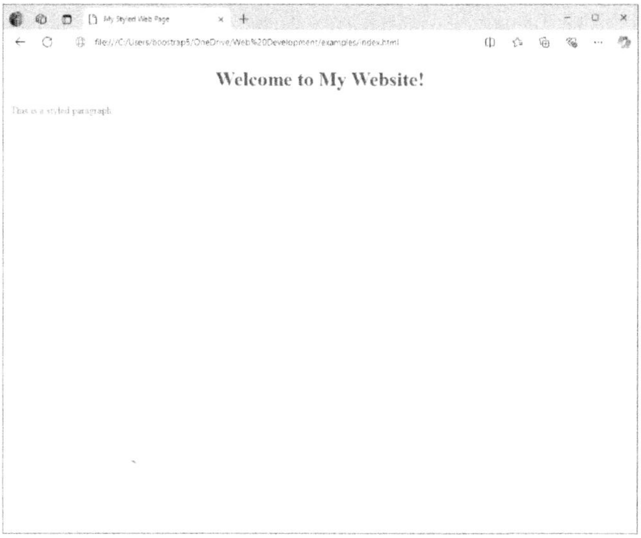

That's it for our quick HTML and CSS review! Remember, this is just a basic overview. There's much more to learn about these languages, but this should give you a good foundation for working with Bootstrap 5.

Now, let's move on to building our first Bootstrap project!

1.5 Your First Bootstrap 5 Project: A Simple Landing Page

Alright, it's time to put our newfound Bootstrap knowledge into action! Let's build a simple landing page—a single-page website that's often used to promote a product, service, or event.

Don't worry if you're a beginner; I'll guide you through every step of the way. We'll use Bootstrap's grid system and some basic components to create a clean and responsive layout.

Setting Up the Structure

1. **Open your index.html file:** This is the file we created earlier in our project folder.

2. **Add the basic HTML structure:** Replace the existing code in your index.html file with the following:

HTML

```
<!DOCTYPE html>
<html lang="en">
<head>
    <meta charset="UTF-8">
    <meta name="viewport" content="width=device-width, initial-
scale=1.0">
    <title>My Landing Page</title>
    <link
href="https://cdn.jsdelivr.net/npm/bootstrap@5.3.0/dist/css/bootstra
p.min.css" rel="stylesheet" integrity="sha384-
9ndCyUaIbzAi2FUVXJi0CjmCapSmO7SnpJef0486qhLnuZ2cdeRhO02iuK6FUUVM"
crossorigin="anonymous">
</head>
<body>

    <script
src="https://cdn.jsdelivr.net/npm/bootstrap@5.3.0/dist/js/bootstrap.
bundle.min.js" integrity="sha384-
geWF76RCwLtnZ8qwWowPQNguL3RmwHVBC9FhGdlKrxdiJJigb/j/68SIy3Te4Bkz"
crossorigin="anonymous"></script>
</body>
</html>
```

This code sets up the basic HTML structure and links the Bootstrap 5 CSS file from a CDN.

Creating the Hero Section

The hero section is typically the first thing visitors see on a landing page. It's a prominent section used to capture attention and convey the main message.

1. **Add a container:** Inside the <body> tag, add a <div> with the class container. This will create a centered area for our content.

2. **Add a heading and paragraph:** Inside the container, add an <h1> heading and a <p> paragraph to introduce your landing page.

3. **Add a button:** Include a <button> element with the class btn btn-primary to create a call to action.

Here's the code:

HTML

```
<div class="container">
    <h1>Welcome to Our Awesome Product!</h1>
    <p>This is a brief description of our amazing product
and why you need it.</p>
    <button class="btn btn-primary">Learn More</button>
</div>
```

Adding More Sections

You can add more sections to your landing page to provide additional information, showcase features, or include testimonials.

For example, let's add a section with three columns:

1. **Create a new div with the class row:** This will create a horizontal row for our columns.
2. **Add three div elements with the class col-md-4:** This will create three equal-width columns on medium-sized screens and larger.

3. **Add content to each column:** Include headings, paragraphs, or images in each column.

Here's the code:

HTML

```
<div class="row">
    <div class="col-md-4">
        <h2>Feature 1</h2>
        <p>Some text about feature 1.</p>
    </div>
    <div class="col-md-4">
        <h2>Feature 2</h2>
        <p>Some text about feature 2.</p>
    </div>
    <div class="col-md-4">
        <h2>Feature 3</h2>
        <p>Some text about feature 3.</p>
    </div>
</div>
```

Running the Code

1. **Save your index.html file.**

2. **Open the file in your web browser.**

You should see your landing page with a hero section and a three-column section. Resize your browser window to see how the layout adapts to different screen sizes.

Congratulations! You've just built your first landing page with Bootstrap 5. It's a simple example, but it demonstrates the power of Bootstrap's grid system and components.

In the next chapter, we'll dive deeper into the grid system and explore its full potential for creating responsive layouts.

CHAPTER 2: MASTERING THE GRID: LAYOUTS AND RESPONSIVE DESIGN

2.1 Understanding Grids: Rows, Columns, and Breakpoints

Alright, let's dive into one of the most powerful features of Bootstrap 5: the grid system! This is where the magic of responsive design really comes to life.

Imagine a city map with streets and avenues forming a neat grid pattern. That's essentially what Bootstrap's grid does for your web pages. It provides a structured framework for arranging your content into rows and columns, making it a breeze to create organized and visually appealing layouts.

Rows and Columns: The Building Blocks

Think of rows as horizontal containers that hold your content. Within each row, you can define columns to divide the space vertically. This allows you to position elements side-by-side or stack them on top of each other, depending on the screen size.

Here's a simple example:

HTML

```html
<div class="container">
  <div class="row">
    <div class="col-md-6">Column 1</div>
    <div class="col-md-6">Column 2</div>
  </div>
</div>
```

In this code:

- container centers your content and provides horizontal padding.
- row creates a horizontal group of columns.
- col-md-6 defines two columns, each taking up half the width of the row on medium-sized screens and larger.

Breakpoints: Adapting to Different Screens

Now, here's where the "responsive" part comes in. Bootstrap uses breakpoints to determine how the layout should adapt to different screen sizes. These breakpoints are predefined width values that trigger changes in the grid's behavior.

Here are the default breakpoints in Bootstrap 5:

- **xs**: Extra small (for phones, less than 576px)
- **sm**: Small (for tablets, 576px and up)
- **md**: Medium (for desktops, 768px and up)
- **lg**: Large (for larger desktops, 992px and up)
- **xl**: Extra large (for extra large desktops, 1200px and up)
- **xxl**: Extra extra large (for extra extra large desktops, 1400px and up)

By using breakpoint prefixes in your column classes (like col-md-6), you can control how the columns are displayed at different screen sizes. For example, col-md-6 will create two columns that each take up half the width of the row on medium-sized screens and larger. On smaller screens, these columns will stack vertically.

The 12-Column Grid

Bootstrap's grid system is based on a 12-column layout. This means that each row can be divided into a maximum of 12 columns. You can use different combinations of column widths to create various layouts.

For example:

- col-md-12 creates a single column that spans the entire width of the row.
- col-md-4 creates three equal-width columns.
- col-md-8 col-md-4 creates two columns, one taking up two-thirds of the row and the other taking up one-third.

Experimenting with the Grid

The best way to understand the grid system is to experiment with it! Try creating different combinations of rows and columns with various breakpoint prefixes. See how the layout changes as you resize your browser window.

Illustration:

Imagine you have a row with three columns, each with a different background color (red, green, and blue). On a large screen, you'll see three equal-width columns side-by-side. As you shrink the browser window, the columns will eventually stack vertically, with red on top, green in the middle, and blue at the bottom.

This dynamic behavior is what makes Bootstrap's grid so powerful for creating responsive layouts that adapt to any screen size.

In the next section, we'll explore how to create basic layouts using the grid system and start building more complex web pages. Let's move on!

2.2 Creating Basic Layouts

Okay, now that we've got a handle on the concepts of rows, columns, and breakpoints, let's put that knowledge to work and start building some basic layouts with Bootstrap 5's grid system.

Think of this as constructing the foundation of your website. We'll start simple, then gradually add more complexity as we go.

Two-Column Layout

One of the most common layouts you'll encounter is the classic two-column design. This is perfect for situations where you want to present content side-by-side, like a sidebar with a main content area.

Here's the HTML code to create a simple two-column layout:

HTML

```
<div class="container">
  <div class="row">
    <div class="col-md-4">
      <h2>Sidebar</h2>
      <p>Some content for the sidebar.</p>
    </div>
    <div class="col-md-8">
      <h2>Main Content</h2>
      <p>This is where the main content of your page goes.</p>
    </div>
  </div>
</div>
```

Let's break it down:

- container: This creates a centered area with horizontal padding for our content.
- row: This establishes a horizontal row to hold our columns.
- col-md-4: This defines the first column, which will take up 4 out of 12 columns on medium-sized screens and larger.

- col-md-8: This defines the second column, taking up the remaining 8 out of 12 columns.

On screens smaller than the "md" breakpoint (less than 768px wide), these columns will automatically stack vertically.

Output:

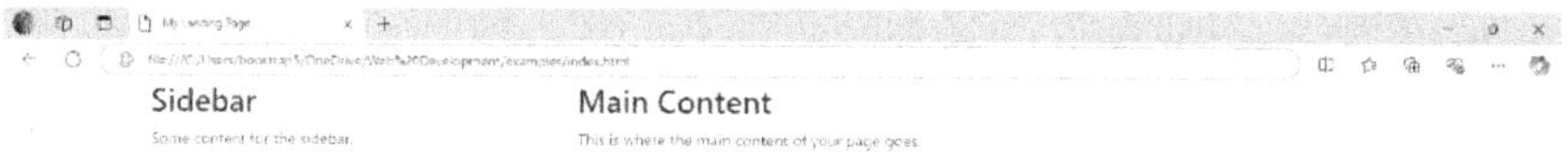

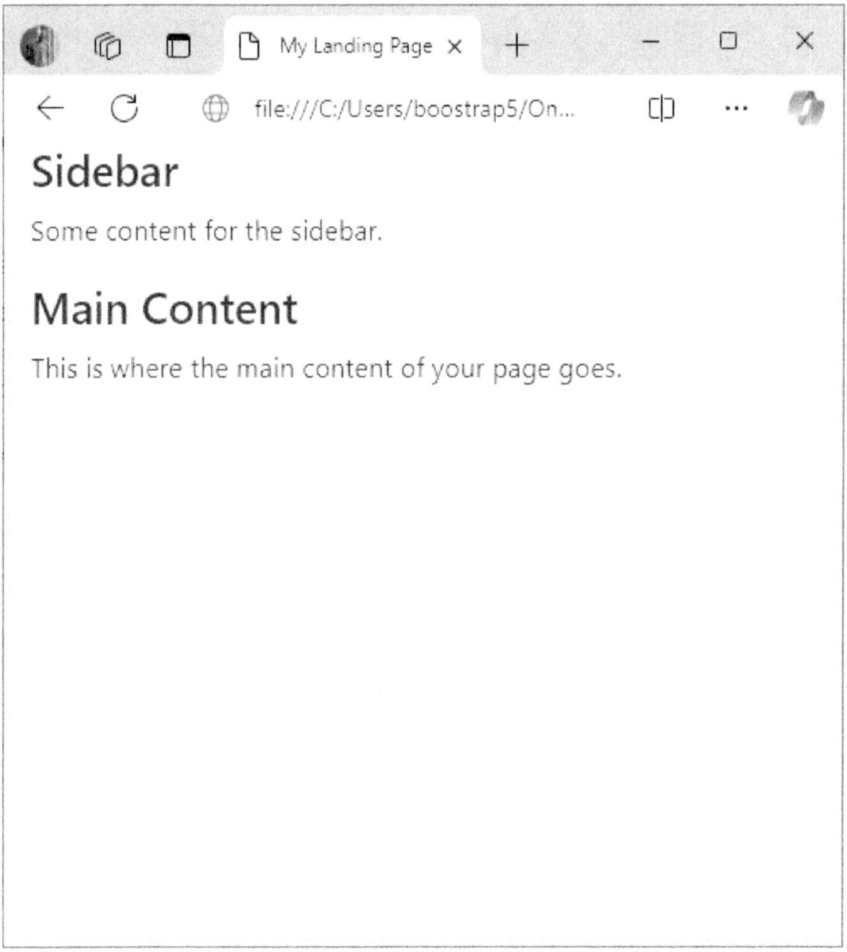
My Landing Page
file:///C:/Users/boostrap5/On...
Sidebar
Some content for the sidebar.
Main Content
This is where the main content of your page goes.

Source Code:

```
<!DOCTYPE html>

<html lang="en">

<head>

  <meta charset="UTF-8">

  <meta name="viewport" content="width=device-width, initial-scale=1.0">

  <title>My Landing Page</title>

  <link href="https://cdn.jsdelivr.net/npm/bootstrap@5.3.0/dist/css/bootstrap.min.css"
rel="stylesheet" integrity="sha384-
9ndCyUaIbzAi2FUVXJi0CjmCapSmO7SnpJef0486qhLnuZ2cdeRhO02iuK6FUUVM"
crossorigin="anonymous">

</head>

<body>

  <div class="container">

    <div class="row">

     <div class="col-md-4">

      <h2>Sidebar</h2>

      <p>Some content for the sidebar.</p>

     </div>

     <div class="col-md-8">

      <h2>Main Content</h2>

      <p>This is where the main content of your page goes.</p>

     </div>

    </div>

   </div>
```

```
    <script
src="https://cdn.jsdelivr.net/npm/bootstrap@5.3.0/dist/js/bootstrap.bundle.min.js"
integrity="sha384-
geWF76RCwLtnZ8qwWowPQNguL3RmwHVBC9FhGdlKrxdiJJigb/j/68SIy3Te4Bkz"
crossorigin="anonymous"></script>

</body>

</html>
```

Three-Column Layout

Need to divide your content into three sections? No problem! Bootstrap's 12-column grid makes it easy.

HTML

```
<div class="container">
  <div class="row">
    <div class="col-md-4">Column 1</div>
    <div class="col-md-4">Column 2</div>
    <div class="col-md-4">Column 3</div>
  </div>
</div>
```

Here, we've used col-md-4 for each column, dividing the row into three equal-width sections.

My Landing Page
Column 1
Column 2
Column 3

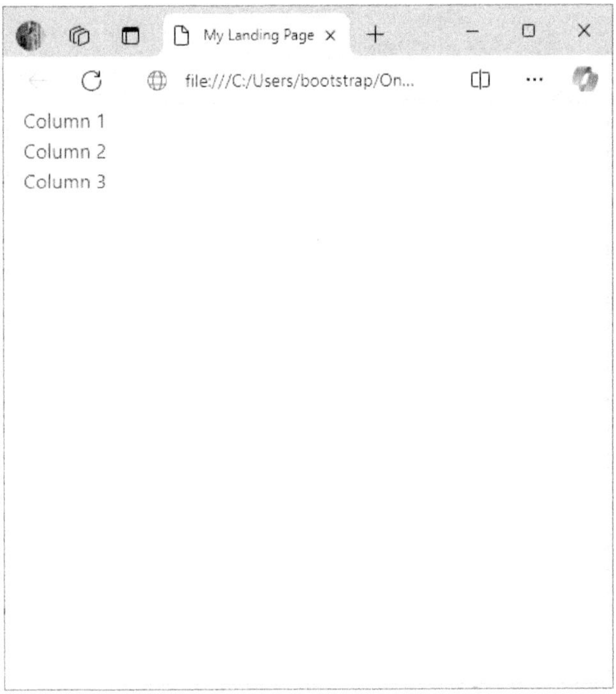
My Landing Page
file:///C:/Users/bootstrap/On...
Column 1
Column 2
Column 3

Combining Columns

You can combine columns of different widths to create more complex layouts. For example:

HTML

```
<div class="container">
  <div class="row">
    <div class="col-md-8">Main Content</div>
    <div class="col-md-4">Sidebar</div>
  </div>
  <div class="row">
    <div class="col-md-3">Column 1</div>
    <div class="col-md-6">Column 2</div>
    <div class="col-md-3">Column 3</div>
  </div>
</div>
```

This code creates two rows:

- The first row has a wider "Main Content" column (8/12) and a narrower "Sidebar" column (4/12).
- The second row has three equal-width columns (3/12 each).

Illustrating the Interface:

Imagine a page with a wider main content area on the left and a narrower sidebar on the right. Below that, you have three smaller columns of equal width.

Experiment and Explore!

These are just a few examples of basic layouts you can create with Bootstrap's grid. The possibilities are truly endless!

I encourage you to experiment with different combinations of rows, columns, and breakpoints to see how you can structure your web pages. Try adding images, text, and other content to your columns to create more engaging layouts.

In the next section, we'll take this a step further and explore how to use the grid system to create truly responsive designs that adapt seamlessly to any screen size. Let's keep building!

2.3 Responsive Design with Grids

Alright, now that we've dipped our toes into the grid system, let's dive deeper and explore how to use it to create truly responsive designs that adapt seamlessly to any screen size.

Remember those breakpoints we talked about earlier? They're the key to making your layouts flexible and adaptable. By using different column classes with breakpoint prefixes, you can control how your content is displayed on various devices.

Stacking Columns

Let's start with a simple example. Say you have a three-column layout:

HTML

```
<div class="container">
  <div class="row">
    <div class="col-md-4">Column 1</div>
    <div class="col-md-4">Column 2</div>
    <div class="col-md-4">Column 3</div>
  </div>
</div>
```

On medium-sized screens and larger, these columns will sit side-by-side, each taking up one-third of the row's width. But what happens on smaller screens?

By default, Bootstrap will automatically stack the columns vertically when the screen width falls below the "md" breakpoint (768px). This ensures that your content remains readable and accessible even on small devices.

Illustrating the Interface:

Imagine those three columns, each with a different background color (red, green, and blue). On a large screen, they're side-by-side. As you shrink the browser window, they'll eventually stack vertically, with red on top, green in the middle, and blue at the bottom.

Controlling Column Behavior

You can fine-tune the responsive behavior of your columns by using different breakpoint prefixes. For example:

- col-sm-6: This column will take up half the row's width on small screens and larger.
- col-lg-3: This column will take up one-quarter of the row's width on large screens and larger.
- col-xl-12: This column will span the entire width of the row on extra-large screens and larger.

You can even combine multiple breakpoint prefixes in a single column class. For example:

HTML

```
<div class="col-sm-6 col-lg-4">
```

This column will take up:

- Half the row's width on small screens and larger.
- One-third of the row's width on large screens and larger.

Creating Dynamic Layouts

By strategically using breakpoint prefixes, you can create dynamic layouts that adapt to different screen sizes in various ways.

For example, you might have a two-column layout on large screens that transforms into a single-column layout on smaller screens. Or you might have a four-column layout that becomes a two-column layout on tablets.

The possibilities are endless! It all depends on your content and how you want it to be displayed on different devices.

Mobile-First Approach

Bootstrap 5 embraces a mobile-first approach to responsive design. This means that the default styles are optimized for small screens. As the screen size increases, you add more specific styles using breakpoint prefixes to enhance the layout for larger displays.

This approach ensures that your website is accessible and user-friendly on all devices, with a focus on providing a great experience on mobile first.

Experiment and Explore!

The best way to master responsive design with grids is to experiment and explore! Try creating different layouts with various breakpoint prefixes and see how they behave on different screen sizes.

Don't be afraid to try out different combinations and see what works best for your content. With a little practice, you'll be creating responsive layouts like a pro in no time!

In the next section, we'll take our grid skills to the next level and explore some advanced features that give you even more control over your layouts. Let's keep going!

2.4 Advanced Grid Features: Offsets, Reordering, and Nesting

Alright, you've mastered the basics of Bootstrap's grid system, building rock-solid layouts like a pro. Now it's time to level up and explore some advanced features that give you even more control and flexibility.

Think of these as your secret weapons for creating truly dynamic and customized web pages.

Offsets: Creating Visual Space

Sometimes, you need to add a little breathing room between your columns. That's where offsets come in handy. Offsets allow you to shift columns to the right by a specified number of columns.

For example, offset-md-4 will shift a column to the right by 4 columns on medium-sized screens and larger.

HTML

```
<div class="container">
  <div class="row">
    <div class="col-md-4 offset-md-4">
      This column is offset by 4 columns.
    </div>
  </div>
</div>
```

Illustrating the Interface:

Imagine a single column centered on the page. It's not touching the left or right edges because it's been offset by 4 columns on each side.

Reordering: Changing the Visual Flow

By default, columns appear in the order they are written in your HTML. But what if you want to change that order for different screen sizes? That's where reordering comes in.

Bootstrap 5 provides classes like order-md-first, order-md-last, and order-md-2 to control the visual order of columns on specific breakpoints.

HTML

```
<div class="container">
  <div class="row">
    <div class="col-md-6 order-md-last">Column 1 (appears last on
medium screens)</div>
    <div class="col-md-6">Column 2</div>
  </div>
</div>
```

Illustrating the Interface:

On large screens, you might have "Column 1" on the left and "Column 2" on the right. But on medium screens, "Column 1" will magically jump to the right side of "Column 2."

Nesting: Creating Grids Within Grids

Want to create more complex layouts with columns within columns? No problem! Bootstrap allows you to nest rows and columns to achieve this.

HTML

```
<div class="container">
  <div class="row">
    <div class="col-md-8">
      <div class="row">
        <div class="col-md-6">Nested Column 1</div>
        <div class="col-md-6">Nested Column 2</div>
      </div>
    </div>
    <div class="col-md-4">Sidebar</div>
  </div>
</div>
```

In this example, the first column of the main row contains another row with two nested columns.

Illustrating the Interface:

Imagine a page with a wider main content area and a narrower sidebar. Within the main content area, you have two smaller columns side-by-side.

Combining Advanced Features

You can combine offsets, reordering, and nesting to create truly intricate and responsive layouts. This gives you incredible flexibility to structure your content in a way that's both visually appealing and user-friendly on all devices.

Experiment and Explore!

As always, the best way to master these advanced grid features is to experiment and explore! Try creating different layouts with offsets, reordering, and nesting. See how they behave on different screen sizes and how they can help you achieve your design goals.

With a little practice, you'll be wielding these advanced grid features like a true Bootstrap 5 ninja!

In the next section, we'll put all our grid knowledge to the test and build a complete responsive marketing page. Get ready to unleash your creativity!

2.5 Project: Building a Responsive Marketing Page

Alright, it's time to put all our grid skills to the test! We're going to build a responsive marketing page for a fictional product—a revolutionary new noise-canceling app called "Hush."

This project will give you hands-on experience with:

- Creating a multi-section layout with rows and columns.
- Using different breakpoints to control responsiveness.
- Incorporating images and text content.
- Adding a call to action.

Get your code editor fired up, and let's get started!

1. Setting up the Structure

First, create a new HTML file named marketing.html in your project folder. Then, add the basic HTML structure and link the Bootstrap 5 CSS file:

```
<!DOCTYPE html>
<html lang="en">
<head>
    <meta charset="UTF-8">
    <meta name="viewport" content="width=device-width, initial-
scale=1.0">
    <title>Hush - Noise-Canceling App</title>
    <link
href="https://cdn.jsdelivr.net/npm/bootstrap@5.3.0/dist/css/bootstra
p.min.css" rel="stylesheet" integrity="sha384-
9ndCyUaIbzAi2FUVXJi0CjmCapSmO7SnpJef0486qhLnuZ2cdeRhO02iuK6FUUVM"
crossorigin="anonymous">
</head>
<body>

    <script
src="https://cdn.jsdelivr.net/npm/bootstrap@5.3.0/dist/js/bootstrap.
bundle.min.js" integrity="sha384-
geWF76RCwLtnZ8qwWowPQNguL3RmwHVBC9FhGdlKrxdiJJigb/j/68SIy3Te4Bkz"
crossorigin="anonymous"></script>
```

```
</body>
</html>
```

2. Building the Hero Section

Let's start with the hero section, the first thing visitors will see.

1. **Add a container**: Inside the <body> tag, add a <div> with the class container.

2. **Create a jumbotron**: Inside the container, add another <div> with the classes jumbotron p-5. This will create a large, prominent section.

3. **Add a heading and paragraph**: Inside the jumbotron, add an <h1> heading and a <p> paragraph to introduce Hush.

4. **Add a button**: Include a <button> with the classes btn btn-primary btn-lg for a prominent call to action.

Here's the code:

HTML

```
<div class="container">
  <div class="jumbotron p-5">
    <h1 class="display-4">Hush: Find Your Focus</h1>
    <p class="lead">Escape the noise and boost your productivity
with our revolutionary noise-canceling app.</p>
    <hr class="my-4">
    <p>Download Hush today and experience the peace and quiet you
deserve.</p>
    <a class="btn btn-primary btn-lg" href="#"
role="button">Download Now</a>
  </div>
</div>
```

3. Showcasing the Features

Next, let's create a section to highlight Hush's key features.

1. Add a new row: Below the jumbotron, add a <div> with the class row.
2. Create three columns: Inside the row, add three <div> elements, each with the class col-md-4.

3. Add content to each column: Include a heading (<h2>), an image (<img>), and a paragraph (<p>) in each column to describe a feature.

Here's the code:

HTML

```
<div class="row">
  <div class="col-md-4">
    <h2>Personalized Soundscapes</h2>
    <img src="images/feature1.jpg" alt="Personalized Soundscapes"
class="img-fluid">
    <p>Create your perfect audio environment with customizable
soundscapes and ambient noises.</p>
  </div>
  <div class="col-md-4">
    <h2>AI-Powered Noise Cancellation</h2>
    <img src="images/feature2.jpg" alt="AI-Powered Noise
Cancellation" class="img-fluid">
    <p>Our advanced AI algorithms intelligently filter out
distractions, leaving you in peace.</p>
  </div>
  <div class="col-md-4">
    <h2>Focus Modes</h2>
    <img src="images/feature3.jpg" alt="Focus Modes" class="img-
fluid">
```

```
    <p>Choose from a variety of focus modes designed to optimize
your concentration and productivity.</p>
  </div>
</div>
```

Important Note: Remember to replace "images/feature1.jpg", "images/feature2.jpg", and "images/feature3.jpg" with the actual paths to your image files. Make sure the images are optimized for web use to keep your page loading fast.

4. Adding a Call to Action Section

Let's add another section to reinforce the call to action.

1. **Create a new row**: Below the features section, add another <div> with the class row.

2. **Add a column**: Inside the row, add a <div> with the class col-md-12.

3. **Add a heading, paragraph, and button**: Include a heading (<h2>), a paragraph (<p>), and a button (<button>) to encourage visitors to download Hush.

Here's the code:

HTML

```
<div class="row">
  <div class="col-md-12 text-center">
    <h2>Ready to Experience the Silence?</h2>
    <p>Download Hush now and start your free trial.</p>
    <a class="btn btn-primary btn-lg" href="#"
role="button">Download Now</a>
  </div>
</div>
```

5. Running the Code

1. Save your marketing.html file.
2. Open the file in your web browser.

You should see a responsive marketing page with a hero section, a features section, and a call to action section. Resize your browser window to see how the layout adapts to different screen sizes.

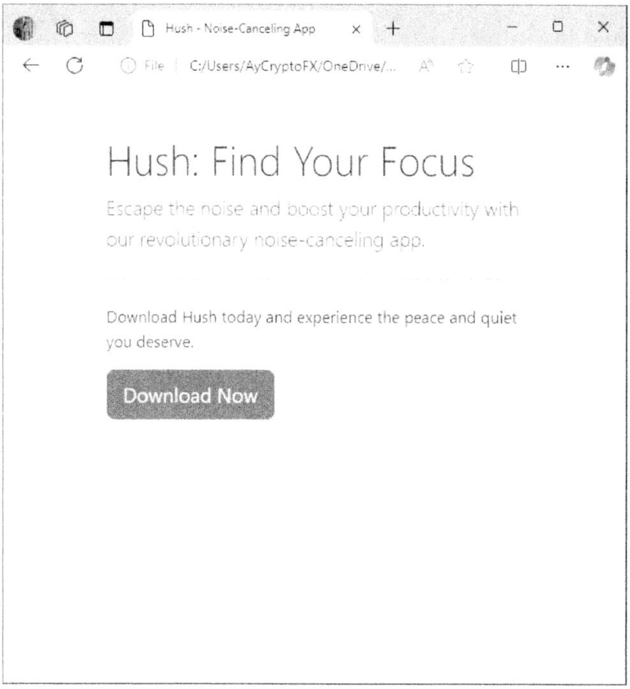
Hush - Noise-Canceling App
File
C:/Users/AyCryptoFX/OneDrive/...
Hush: Find Your Focus
Escape the noise and boost your productivity with our revolutionary noise-canceling app.
Download Hush today and experience the peace and quiet you deserve.
Download Now

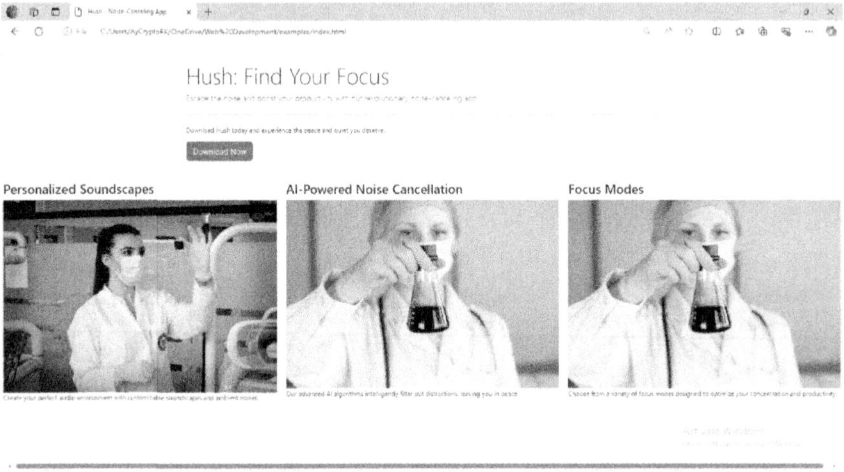

Illustrating the Interface:

Imagine a visually appealing page with a large hero section featuring a captivating heading, a compelling description of Hush, and a prominent "Download Now" button. Below that, you see three columns showcasing the app's key features with images and text. Finally, there's a centered call to action encouraging visitors to download the app.

As you resize the browser window, the three feature columns will gracefully stack on top of each other on smaller screens, ensuring a clean and readable layout on all devices.

Congratulations! You've just built a responsive marketing page with Bootstrap 5. This project demonstrates how to combine the grid system with various Bootstrap components to create a professional and engaging web page.

Keep experimenting with different layouts, content, and styles to further enhance your Bootstrap skills. In the next chapter, we'll dive into the world of Bootstrap 5 components and explore the wide range of pre-designed elements you can use to build your websites.

CHAPTER 3: ESSENTIAL BOOTSTRAP 5 COMPONENTS

3.1 Typography and Text Utilities

Alright, let's dive into the world of Bootstrap 5 components! These pre-designed building blocks are the heart and soul of the framework, allowing you to quickly assemble and style your web pages with ease.

We'll start with the fundamentals: typography and text utilities. These might seem like small details, but they play a huge role in creating a visually appealing and user-friendly website. After all, what good is content if it's difficult to read or looks messy?

Headings and Paragraphs

Bootstrap provides predefined styles for headings (<h1> to <h6>) and paragraphs (<p>) that ensure consistency and readability. These styles are based on a carefully chosen font family, font sizes, and line heights.

Here's a quick example:

HTML

```
<h1>This is a heading</h1>
<p>This is a paragraph of text.</p>
```

Illustrating the Interface:

Imagine a page with a large, bold heading at the top, followed by a paragraph of text with a comfortable line spacing. The font is clean and easy to read, making the content inviting and acccssible.

Display Headings

For those times when you need a heading to really stand out, Bootstrap offers display headings. These are larger and more prominent than standard headings, perfect for grabbing attention.

HTML

```
<h1 class="display-1">Display 1</h1>
<h2 class="display-2">Display 2</h2>
<h3 class="display-3">Display 3</h2>
<h4 class="display-4">Display 4</h4>
```

Illustrating the Interface:

Picture those headings increasing in size dramatically, creating a visual hierarchy that guides the reader's eye.

Text Alignment

Need to align your text to the left, center, or right? Bootstrap's text alignment utilities make it a snap.

HTML

```
<p class="text-start">Left-aligned text.</p>
<p class="text-center">Centered text.</p>
<p class="text-end">Right-aligned text.</p>
```

Illustrating the Interface:

Imagine three paragraphs of text, each aligned differently. The first paragraph is neatly aligned to the left margin, the second is perfectly centered on the page, and the third is flush against the right margin.

Text Wrapping and Overflow

Sometimes, you need to control how text wraps within its container or handle situations where text might overflow. Bootstrap provides utilities for that too!

HTML

```
<div style="width: 100px;">
  <p class="text-wrap">This text will wrap within the container.</p>
</div>
<div style="width: 100px;">
  <p class="text-nowrap">This text will not wrap and will overflow
the container.</p>
</div>
```

Illustrating the Interface:

In the first div, the text neatly wraps to the next line when it reaches the edge of the container. In the second div, the text extends beyond the container's boundary, potentially causing a horizontal scrollbar.

Text Transform

Want to change the case of your text? Bootstrap's text transform utilities can help.

HTML

```
<p class="text-lowercase">lowercase text</p>

<p class="text-uppercase">UPPERCASE TEXT</p>

<p class="text-capitalize">Capitalized Text</p>
```

Illustrating the Interface:

The first paragraph appears in all lowercase letters, the second in all uppercase, and the third with the first letter of each word capitalized.

Font Weight and Style

Need to bold or italicize your text? Bootstrap's got you covered.

HTML

```
<p class="fw-bold">Bold text</p>
<p class="fw-bolder">Bolder text</p>
<p class="fw-normal">Normal weight text</p>
<p class="fw-light">Light weight text</p>
<p class="fst-italic">Italic text</p>
```

Illustrating the Interface:

Imagine the first paragraph appearing in bold, the second even bolder, the third with a regular weight, the fourth lighter than normal, and the fifth elegantly italicized.

Line Height

Control the spacing between lines of text with Bootstrap's line height utilities.

HTML

```
<p class="lh-1">Line height 1</p>
<p class="lh-sm">Small line height</p>
<p class="lh-base">Base line height</p>
<p class="lh-lg">Large line height</p>
```

Illustrating the Interface:

Notice how the spacing between the lines of text changes in each paragraph, creating different visual rhythms.

Experiment and Explore!

These are just a few of the many typography and text utilities that Bootstrap 5 offers. I encourage you to experiment with them and see how they can enhance the readability and visual appeal of your web pages.

Remember, typography plays a crucial role in user experience. By using Bootstrap's text utilities effectively, you can create content that is not only informative but also enjoyable to read.

In the next section, we'll move on to exploring another essential set of Bootstrap components: buttons!

3.2 Buttons and Button Groups

Alright, let's move on to another essential building block in Bootstrap 5: buttons! These interactive elements are crucial for triggering actions, navigating between pages, and generally making your website more dynamic.

Bootstrap provides a wide variety of button styles, sizes, and states to help you create visually appealing and functional buttons that fit seamlessly into your design.

Basic Buttons

Creating a basic button with Bootstrap is as simple as adding the class btn to a <button> element:

HTML

```
<button class="btn">Click me</button>
```

This will give you a basic button with a default style. But Bootstrap offers much more than just that!

Button Styles

You can apply different styles to your buttons using contextual classes:

- btn-primary: Blue button (often used for the main call to action)
- btn-secondary: Gray button (for less prominent actions)
- btn-success: Green button (for successful actions)
- btn-danger: Red button (for destructive actions)
- btn-warning: Yellow button (for warnings or cautions)
- btn-info: Light blue button (for informational actions)
- btn-light: Light gray button
- btn-dark: Dark gray button
- btn-link: Link-style button (appears like a regular hyperlink)

Here's an example:

HTML

```
<button class="btn btn-primary">Primary</button>
<button class="btn btn-
secondary">Secondary</button>
<button class="btn btn-success">Success</button>
```

Illustrating the Interface:

Imagine three buttons side-by-side. The first is a bold blue, the second a more subtle gray, and the third a vibrant green.

Button Sizes

You can also control the size of your buttons:

- btn-sm: Small button
- btn-lg: Large button

HTML

```
<button class="btn btn-primary btn-sm">Small</button>
<button class="btn btn-primary">Normal</button>
<button class="btn btn-primary btn-lg">Large</button>
```

Illustrating the Interface:

Picture three buttons of varying sizes. The first is compact and subtle, the second is a standard size, and the third is large and prominent.

Button States

Bootstrap provides classes to style buttons in different states:

- active: For a button that is currently active (e.g., a toggle button)
- disabled: For a button that is disabled

HTML

```
<button class="btn btn-primary active">Active</button>
<button class="btn btn-primary" disabled>Disabled</button>
```

Illustrating the Interface:

The first button appears pressed down, indicating its active state. The second button is grayed out, visually conveying that it cannot be clicked.

Button Groups

Button groups allow you to group multiple buttons together, creating a more organized and visually appealing interface.

HTML

```
<div class="btn-group" role="group" aria-label="Basic
example">
  <button type="button" class="btn btn-
primary">Left</button>
  <button type="button" class="btn btn-
primary">Middle</button>
  <button type="button" class="btn btn-
primary">Right</button>
</div>
```

Illustrating the Interface:

Imagine three blue buttons grouped together, visually connected with rounded corners.

Advanced Button Features

Bootstrap offers even more advanced button features, such as:

- Toggle buttons: Create buttons that can be toggled on and off.
- Checkbox and radio buttons: Style checkboxes and radio buttons to look like buttons.

- Dropdown buttons: Combine buttons with dropdown menus for more complex actions.

We'll explore these advanced features in later chapters.

Experiment and Explore!

Buttons are essential elements in any web application. Bootstrap 5 provides a comprehensive set of tools for creating stylish and functional buttons that enhance the user experience.

I encourage you to experiment with different button styles, sizes, states, and groups to see how they can bring your web pages to life.

In the next section, we'll move on to another crucial set of components: navigation bars!

3.3 Navigation Bars and Navs

Alright, let's move on to another crucial component in web design: navigation bars! These are the roadmaps of your website, guiding users to different sections and pages.

Bootstrap 5 provides a flexible and powerful navigation bar component, often referred to as a "navbar," that you can easily customize to fit your website's design and structure.

Basic Navbar Structure

Here's the basic HTML structure of a Bootstrap navbar:

HTML

```
<nav class="navbar navbar-expand-lg navbar-light bg-light">
  <div class="container-fluid">
    <a class="navbar-brand" href="#">Navbar</a>
    <button class="navbar-toggler" type="button" data-bs-
toggle="collapse" data-bs-target="#navbarNav" aria-
controls="navbarNav" aria-expanded="false" aria-
label="Toggle navigation">
      <span class="navbar-toggler-icon"></span>
    </button>
    <div class="collapse navbar-collapse" id="navbarNav">
```

```
      <ul class="navbar-nav">
        <li class="nav-item">
          <a class="nav-link active" aria-current="page"
href="#">Home</a>
        </li>
        <li class="nav-item">
          <a class="nav-link" href="#">Features</a>
        </li>
        <li class="nav-item">
          <a class="nav-link" href="#">Pricing</a>
        </li>
        <li class="nav-item">
          <a class="nav-link disabled" href="#" tabindex="-
1" aria-disabled="true">Disabled</a>
        </li>
      </ul>
    </div>
  </div>
</nav>
```

Let's break it down:

- **<nav>:** The main container for the navbar.
- **navbar:** The base class for the navbar.
- **navbar-expand-lg:** This class makes the navbar responsive, collapsing the navigation links into a dropdown menu on smaller screens (in this case, "lg" means large screens and below).
- **navbar-light bg-light:** This adds a light color scheme to the navbar.
- **container-fluid:** This ensures the navbar spans the full width of the viewport.
- **navbar-brand:** This is typically used for your website's logo or name.
- **navbar-toggler:** This is the button that appears on smaller screens to toggle the collapsed navigation menu.

- **navbar-collapse:** This is the container for the navigation links that collapses on smaller screens.
- **navbar-nav:** This is the list of navigation links.
- **nav-item:** Each navigation link is wrapped in a list item.
- **nav-link:** This class styles the navigation links.

Navbar Variations

Bootstrap offers several variations of the navbar:

- **Color schemes:** Use navbar-light for a light background or navbar-dark for a dark background.
- **Positioning:** Use fixed-top, fixed-bottom, or sticky-top to position the navbar at the top or bottom of the viewport or make it "sticky" as the user scrolls.
- **Content:** Add various elements to the navbar, such as forms, buttons, or dropdown menus.

Navs

Navs are similar to navbars but are more general-purpose. They can be used for navigation menus, tabs, pills, or any other list of links.

Here's an example of a basic nav:

HTML

```
<ul class="nav">
  <li class="nav-item">
    <a class="nav-link active" aria-current="page"
href="#">Active</a>
  </li>
  <li class="nav-item">
    <a class="nav-link" href="#">Link</a>
  </li>
  <li class="nav-item">
    <a class="nav-link" href="#">Link</a>
  </li>
  <li class="nav-item">
    <a class="nav-link disabled" href="#" tabindex="-1"
aria-disabled="true">Disabled</a>
  </li>
</ul>
```

Nav Variations

Bootstrap provides different styles for navs:

- **Tabs:** Use nav-tabs for a tabbed interface.
- **Pills:** Use nav-pills for a pill-style navigation.
- **Vertical alignment:** Use flex-column to align nav links vertically.
- **Justification:** Use justify-content-center, justify-content-end, etc. to justify nav links within the container.

Illustrating the Interface

Imagine a website with a horizontal bar at the top. This bar contains the website's logo on the left and a list of links on the right (e.g., "Home," "About," "Contact"). On smaller screens, the links collapse into a dropdown menu that can be toggled with a button.

This is a typical example of a Bootstrap navbar. Navs, on the other hand, can be used for various purposes, such as creating a vertical list of links in a sidebar or a set of tabs to organize content.

Experiment and Explore!

Navigation is a crucial aspect of any website. Bootstrap 5 provides flexible and customizable navbar and nav components that make it easy to create user-friendly navigation experiences.

I encourage you to experiment with different navbar and nav variations, adding your own content and styles to create navigation that perfectly suits your website's needs.

In the next section, we'll move on to exploring another essential set of components: forms!

3.4 Forms and Form Controls

Alright, let's talk about forms! These essential elements are the workhorses of web applications, allowing users to interact with your site by submitting data, providing feedback, or making choices.

Bootstrap 5 provides a comprehensive set of tools for creating stylish and functional forms that are easy to use and integrate seamlessly into your website's design.

Basic Form Structure

Here's the basic HTML structure of a Bootstrap form:

HTML

```
<form>
  <div class="mb-3">
    <label for="exampleInputEmail1" class="form-label">Email
address</label>
    <input type="email" class="form-control" id="exampleInputEmail1"
aria-describedby="emailHelp">
    <div id="emailHelp" class="form-text">We'll never share your
email with anyone else.</div>
```

```
  </div>
  <div class="mb-3">
    <label for="exampleInputPassword1" class="form-
label">Password</label>
    <input type="password" class="form-control"
id="exampleInputPassword1">
  </div>
  <div class="mb-3 form-check">
    <input type="checkbox" class="form-check-input"
id="exampleCheck1">
    <label class="form-check-label" for="exampleCheck1">Check me
out</label>
  </div>
  <button type="submit" class="btn btn-primary">Submit</button>
</form>
```

Let's break it down:

- **<form>:** The main container for the form.
- **mb-3:** This class adds a margin to the bottom of each form group.
- **<label>:** Provides a label for the input field.
- **form-label:** Styles the label.

- **<input>:** The actual input field where the user enters data.
- **form-control:** Styles the input field.
- **form-text:** Used for providing additional information or help text below the input field.
- **form-check:** Used for styling checkboxes and radio buttons.

Input Types

Bootstrap styles a variety of input types:

- **text:** For single-line text input.
- **email:** For email addresses.
- **password:** For passwords (obscures the input).
- **number:** For numeric input.
- **date:** For date input.

- **textarea:** For multi-line text input.
- **select:** For dropdown menus.
- **checkbox:** For checkboxes.
- **radio:** For radio buttons.
- **file:** For file uploads.

Form Layout

Bootstrap provides classes for creating different form layouts:

- **Vertical form (default):** Input fields are stacked vertically.
- **Horizontal form:** Labels and input fields are arranged horizontally.
- **Inline form:** Form controls are displayed inline.

Form Validation

Bootstrap provides styles for visually indicating form validation states:

- **is-valid:** For successful validation.
- **is-invalid:** For failed validation.

Bootstrap's form styles ensure that the form looks consistent and professional, with clear labels and input fields that are easy to interact with.

In the next section, we'll move on to exploring another important set of components: alerts, badges, and progress bars!

3.5 Alerts, Badges, and Progress Bars

Alright, let's explore a trio of Bootstrap components that are great for providing feedback, highlighting information, and displaying progress: alerts, badges, and progress bars.

These components might seem small, but they can significantly enhance the user experience by providing visual cues and conveying important information in a clear and concise way.

Alerts: Catching Attention

Alerts are those eye-catching boxes that you often see on websites to provide feedback messages, warnings, or notifications. Bootstrap offers a variety of alert styles to match different situations.

Here's a basic alert:

HTML

```
<div class="alert alert-primary" role="alert">
  A simple primary alert—check it out!
</div>
```

This code creates a blue alert box with the text "A simple primary alert—check it out!"

Alert Styles

Bootstrap provides several contextual classes to style alerts:

- alert-primary: Blue alert
- alert-secondary: Gray alert
- alert-success: Green alert (for success messages)
- alert-danger: Red alert (for error messages)
- alert-warning: Yellow alert (for warnings)
- alert-info: Light blue alert (for informational messages)
- alert-light: Light gray alert
- alert-dark: Dark gray alert

Dismissing Alerts

You can make alerts dismissible by adding a close button:

HTML

```
<div class="alert alert-warning alert-dismissible fade show"
role="alert">
  <strong>Holy guacamole!</strong> You should check in on some of
those fields below.
  <button type="button" class="btn-close" data-bs-dismiss="alert"
aria-label="Close"></button>
</div>
```

This alert includes a close button that allows the user to dismiss it.

Illustrating the Interface

Imagine a blue box at the top of a form that says "Successfully submitted!" This is a typical example of a success alert. Or, picture a yellow box warning the user that some fields are required.

Alerts are great for providing immediate feedback and drawing attention to important information.

Badges: Highlighting Information

Badges are those little labels that you often see on buttons or navigation items to highlight notifications, counts, or status.

Here's a basic badge:

HTML

```html
<span class="badge bg-primary">Primary</span>
```

This code creates a blue badge with the text "Primary."

Badge Styles

You can apply different styles to badges using contextual classes, just like alerts. You can also use badge-pill to give badges a rounded pill shape.

Illustrating the Interface

Imagine a notification icon with a small red badge that says "3" to indicate three unread notifications. Or, picture a shopping cart icon with a green badge that says "2" to show two items in the cart.

Badges are a subtle but effective way to highlight information and draw attention to specific elements.

Progress Bars: Showing Completion

Progress bars visually represent the progress of a task or process.

Here's a basic progress bar:

HTML

```
<div class="progress">
  <div class="progress-bar" role="progressbar" style="width: 25%;"
aria-valuenow="25" aria-valuemin="0" aria-valuemax="100"></div>
</div>
```

This code creates a progress bar that is 25% complete.

Progress Bar Styles

You can apply different styles to progress bars using contextual classes, just like alerts and badges. You can also use progress-bar-striped to add stripes and progress-bar-animated to create an animated effect.

Illustrating the Interface

Imagine a horizontal bar that gradually fills with green as a file uploads. Or, picture a progress bar with stripes that animates while a task is being processed.

Progress bars provide a visual representation of progress, keeping users informed and engaged.

Experiment and Explore!

Alerts, badges, and progress bars are valuable tools for enhancing user feedback and conveying information in a visually appealing way.

In the next section, we'll move on to exploring another essential set of components: forms!

3.6 Project: Creating a Stylish Registration Form

Alright, let's put our form-building skills to the test! In this project, we'll create a stylish registration form for our fictional "Hush" noise-canceling app. We'll combine Bootstrap's form controls, layout options, and validation styles to craft a user-friendly and visually appealing registration experience.

Get your code editor ready, and let's dive in!

1. Setting up the Structure

1. Create a new HTML file: Create a new file named registration.html in your project folder.

2. Add the basic HTML structure: Include the basic HTML structure and link the Bootstrap 5 CSS file:

```
<!DOCTYPE html>
<html lang="en">
<head>
    <meta charset="UTF-8">
```

```
    <meta name="viewport" content="width=device-width, initial-scale=1.0">
    <title>Hush - Register</title>
    <link href="https://cdn.jsdelivr.net/npm/bootstrap@5.3.0/dist/css/bootstrap.min.css" rel="stylesheet" integrity="sha384-9ndCyUaIbzAi2FUVXJi0CjmCapSmO7SnpJef0486qhLnuZ2cdeRhO02iuK6FUUVM" crossorigin="anonymous">
</head>
<body>

    <script src="https://cdn.jsdelivr.net/npm/bootstrap@5.3.0/dist/js/bootstrap.bundle.min.js" integrity="sha384-geWF76RCwLtnZ8qwWowPQNguL3RmwHVBC9FhGdlKrxdiJJigb/j/68SIy3Te4Bkz" crossorigin="anonymous"></script>
</body>
</html>
```

2. Creating the Form Container

1. Add a container: Inside the <body> tag, add a <div> with the class container. This will center our form on the page.

2. Add a heading: Inside the container, add an <h2> heading to title the form (e.g., "Register for Hush").

3. Building the Form

Now, let's create the form itself. We'll use Bootstrap's form controls and layout options to structure the input fields.

```
<div class="container">
  <h2>Register for Hush</h2>
  <form>
    <div class="mb-3">
      <label for="name" class="form-label">Full Name</label>
      <input type="text" class="form-control" id="name"
placeholder="Enter your full name">
    </div>
    <div class="mb-3">
      <label for="email" class="form-label">Email address</label>
      <input type="email" class="form-control" id="email"
placeholder="Enter your email">
    </div>
    <div class="mb-3">
      <label for="password" class="form-label">Password</label>
      <input type="password" class="form-control" id="password"
placeholder="Enter your password">
    </div>
    <div class="mb-3 form-check">
      <input type="checkbox" class="form-check-input" id="terms">
```

```
      <label class="form-check-label" for="terms">I agree to the terms and conditions</label>
    </div>
    <button type="submit" class="btn btn-primary">Register</button>
  </form>
</div>
```

This code creates a form with fields for full name, email address, and password, along with a checkbox for agreeing to terms and conditions.

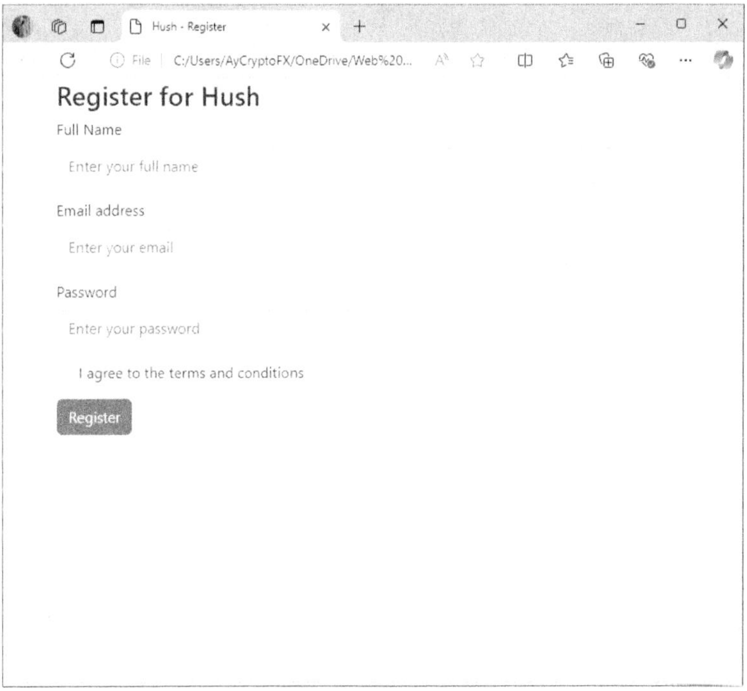

4. Adding Validation Styles

Let's add some visual feedback to indicate validation states. We'll use Bootstrap's is-valid and is-invalid classes.

HTML

```
<div class="mb-3">
  <label for="name" class="form-label">Full Name</label>
  <input type="text" class="form-control is-valid" id="name"
placeholder="Enter your full name">
  <div class="valid-feedback">
    Looks good!
  </div>
</div>
<div class="mb-3">
  <label for="email" class="form-label">Email address</label>
  <input   type="email"   class="form-control   is-invalid"
id="email" placeholder="Enter your email">
  <div class="invalid-feedback">
    Please provide a valid email.
  </div>
</div>
```

In this example, the "Full Name" field is marked as valid with a green checkmark, while the "Email address" field is marked as invalid with a red "x."

Important Note: This is just a visual representation of validation. You'll need to add JavaScript code to actually validate the form data.

5. Running the Code

1. Save your registration.html file.
2. Open the file in your web browser.

You should see a stylish registration form with clearly labeled input fields, a checkbox for terms and conditions, and a submit button. The validation styles provide visual feedback to the user.

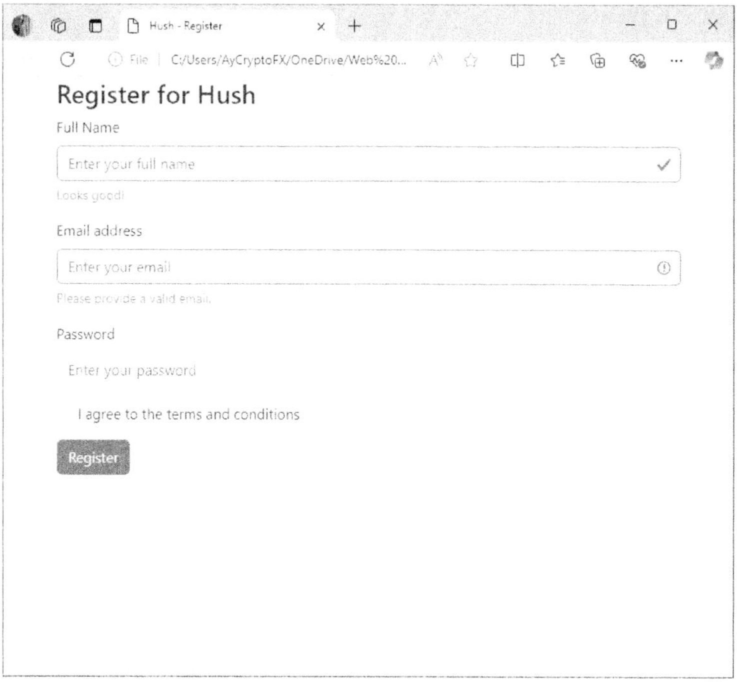
Hush - Register
C:/Users/AyCryptoFX/OneDrive/Web%20...
Register for Hush
Full Name
Enter your full name
Looks good!
Email address
Enter your email
Please provide a valid email.
Password
Enter your password
I agree to the terms and conditions
Register

Source Code:

```
<!DOCTYPE html>
<html lang="en">
<head>
  <meta charset="UTF-8">
  <meta name="viewport" content="width=device-width, initial-scale=1.0">
  <title>Hush - Register</title>
  <link href="https://cdn.jsdelivr.net/npm/bootstrap@5.3.0/dist/css/bootstrap.min.css"
rel="stylesheet" integrity="sha384-
9ndCyUaIbzAi2FUVXJi0CjmCapSmO7SnpJef0486qhLnuZ2cdeRhO02iuK6FUUVM"
crossorigin="anonymous">
</head>
<body>

  <div class="container">
   <h2>Register for Hush</h2>
   <form>

    <div class="mb-3">
    <label for="name" class="form-label">Full Name</label>
    <input type="text" class="form-control is-valid" id="name" placeholder="Enter your full
name">
    <div class="valid-feedback">
      Looks good!
    </div>
    </div>
    <div class="mb-3">
    <label for="email" class="form-label">Email address</label>
    <input type="email" class="form-control is-invalid" id="email" placeholder="Enter your
email">
```

```
      <div class="invalid-feedback">
        Please provide a valid email.
      </div>
      </div>

      <div class="mb-3">
       <label for="password" class="form-label">Password</label>
       <input type="password" class="form-control" id="password" placeholder="Enter your
password">
      </div>
      <div class="mb-3 form-check">
       <input type="checkbox" class="form-check-input" id="terms">
       <label class="form-check-label" for="terms">I agree to the terms and
conditions</label>
      </div>
      <button type="submit" class="btn btn-primary">Register</button>
    </form>
   </div>

   <script
src="https://cdn.jsdelivr.net/npm/bootstrap@5.3.0/dist/js/bootstrap.bundle.min.js"
integrity="sha384-
geWF76RCwLtnZ8qwWowPQNguL3RmwHVBC9FhGdlKrxdiJJigb/j/68SIy3Te4Bkz"
crossorigin="anonymous"></script>
</body>
</html>
```

Illustrating the Interface:

Imagine a clean and organized form with a prominent heading that says "Register for Hush." Below the heading, you see input fields for "Full Name," "Email address," and "Password." Each field has a label and a placeholder text. There's also a checkbox with the label "I agree to the terms and conditions." Finally, there's a blue "Register" button at the bottom.

The "Full Name" field has a green checkmark next to it, indicating that the input is valid. The "Email address" field has a red "x" next to it, indicating an invalid entry.

Congratulations! You've just created a stylish and functional registration form with Bootstrap 5. This project demonstrates how to combine form controls, layout options, and validation styles to create a user-friendly registration experience.

Keep experimenting with different form elements, styles, and validation techniques to further enhance your Bootstrap skills. In the next chapter, we'll dive into the world of Bootstrap 5 components and explore the wide range of pre-designed elements you can use to build your websites.

CHAPTER 4: CUSTOMIZATION WITH CSS AND SASS

4.1 Understanding Bootstrap 5's CSS Architecture

Okay, so far, we've been using Bootstrap 5 "out of the box," taking advantage of its pre-designed styles and components. But what if you want to give your website a unique look and feel? That's where customization comes in, and understanding Bootstrap's CSS architecture is the first step.

Think of Bootstrap's CSS as a well-organized wardrobe. It has different sections for different types of clothes: shirts, pants, shoes, accessories. You can mix and match these items to create various outfits, but you can also customize them further by altering their colors, patterns, or fit.

Similarly, Bootstrap's CSS is organized into several key areas:

1. **Reboot**: This is the foundation of Bootstrap's CSS. It resets and normalizes default browser styles, creating a consistent baseline for your web pages across different browsers. Think of it as ironing out all the wrinkles and inconsistencies before you start styling your clothes.

2. **Utilities**: These are the small, reusable CSS classes that you can apply to individual elements to quickly style them. They control things like margins, padding, colors, text alignment, and display properties. Think of them as the quick and easy accessories you can use to add a touch of flair to your outfit.

3. **Components**: These are the larger, pre-designed building blocks of Bootstrap, like buttons, navbars, and forms. They combine HTML, CSS, and sometimes JavaScript to create reusable UI elements. Think of them as the complete outfits in your wardrobe, ready to wear with minimal adjustments.

4. **Layout**: This section handles the overall layout of your web page, including the grid system, flexbox utilities, and responsive design features. Think of it as the blueprint for how your clothes will be arranged and displayed.

The Power of Sass

Bootstrap 5 is built with Sass, a powerful CSS preprocessor that adds features like variables, mixins, and functions to your CSS workflow. This makes it much easier to customize Bootstrap's styles and create your own themes.

Think of Sass as a tailor who can help you customize your clothes to fit perfectly. You can provide the tailor with specific measurements and preferences, and they'll adjust the clothes accordingly.

Similarly, with Sass, you can:

- Change variables: Modify Bootstrap's default colors, fonts, and spacing by adjusting Sass variables.
- Create mixins: Define reusable blocks of CSS code to apply common styles to multiple elements.
- Use functions: Perform calculations and manipulate values within your CSS.

Customizing Bootstrap

There are two main ways to customize Bootstrap 5 with Sass:

1. Override variables: Create a custom Sass file and import Bootstrap's Sass files. Then, override the default variables with your own values.
2. Create a custom theme: Use Bootstrap's _variables.scss file as a starting point and customize the variables to create a unique theme.

We'll explore both of these approaches in more detail in the following sections.

Illustrating the Architecture

Imagine a house being built. The reboot is like the foundation, providing a stable base. The utilities are like the bricks and mortar, used to build individual walls and features. The components are like pre-fabricated rooms, such as the kitchen or bathroom. And the layout is like the overall floor plan, determining how the rooms are arranged.

Sass is like the architect who can modify the blueprint and customize the materials to create a unique and personalized house.

Understanding the architecture is key to effective customization.

By knowing how Bootstrap's CSS is organized and how Sass works, you can confidently make changes to the framework and create websites that truly reflect your vision.

In the next section, we'll dive into the practical aspects of customizing Bootstrap 5 with CSS and Sass. Get ready to unleash your creativity!

4.2 Overriding Default Styles

Alright, let's get our hands dirty with some customization! While Bootstrap 5 provides a fantastic foundation with its default styles, you'll often want to tweak things to match your specific design vision.

Think of it like this: you buy a suit off the rack, but it needs some alterations to fit you perfectly. You might adjust the sleeve length, take in the waist, or add a custom lining. Similarly, you can override Bootstrap's default styles to create a website that truly reflects your brand or project requirements.

The Cascade: CSS's Secret Weapon

Before we dive into the how-to, let's briefly touch on a fundamental concept in CSS: the cascade. This is what determines which styles "win" when multiple rules apply to the same element.

In general, styles defined later in your CSS file will override earlier styles. This means you can use this principle to your advantage when customizing Bootstrap. By adding your custom styles after the Bootstrap CSS file, you can override its defaults.

Methods for Overriding Styles

Here are the main ways to override Bootstrap's default styles:

1. External Stylesheet:

- **Create a separate CSS file**: Create a new CSS file in your project folder (e.g., custom.css).
- **Link it after Bootstrap**: In your HTML file, link your custom CSS file after the Bootstrap CSS file. This ensures that your styles take precedence.

HTML

```html
<link
href="https://cdn.jsdelivr.net/npm/bootstrap@5.3.0/dist/css/bootstra
p.min.css"          rel="stylesheet"          integrity="sha384-
9ndCyUaIbzAi2FUVXJi0CjmCapSmO7SnpJef0486qhLnuZ2cdeRhO02iuK6FUUVM"
crossorigin="anonymous">
<link rel="stylesheet" href="custom.css">
```

- Write your custom styles: In your custom.css file, write CSS rules to override Bootstrap's defaults. Be as specific as possible with your selectors to target the elements you want to modify.

CSS

```
/* Change the background color of primary buttons */
.btn-primary {
  background-color: #007bff; /* Your custom color */
}
```

2. Internal Stylesheet:

- Add a <style> tag: In the <head> section of your HTML file, add a <style> tag.
- Write your custom styles: Inside the <style> tag, write your CSS rules to override Bootstrap's defaults. Again, be specific with your selectors.

HTML

```
<head>
  <style>
    /* Change the font size of headings */
    h1, h2, h3, h4, h5, h6 {
      font-size: 1.2rem; /* Your custom font size */
    }
  </style>
</head>
```

3. Inline Styles (Not Recommended):

- Use the style attribute: Add the style attribute to an HTML element and write your CSS rules directly within it.

HTML
```
<p style="color: red;">This paragraph will be red.</p>
```

- Note: While inline styles offer the highest specificity, they are generally not recommended for extensive customization because they mix CSS with your HTML and can make your code harder to maintain.

Specificity: Winning the CSS Battle

When overriding styles, remember that specificity matters. More specific selectors will take precedence over less specific ones.

For example, a class selector (.my-class) is more specific than an element selector (p). And an ID selector (#my-element) is more specific than a class selector.

If you're having trouble overriding a particular style, try using a more specific selector or the !important declaration (use with caution!).

Illustrating the Override

Imagine you have a Bootstrap button with the class btn-primary. By default, it's blue. But you want it to be green. You can create a CSS rule in your custom stylesheet:

```css
CSS
.btn-primary {
  background-color: green;
}
```

This rule will override Bootstrap's default blue background color and make your button green.

Experiment and Explore!

Overriding default styles is a fundamental skill in Bootstrap customization.

I encourage you to experiment with different methods of overriding styles and see how you can tailor Bootstrap to your specific needs.

In the next section, we'll take customization to the next level by exploring the power of Sass variables and mixins. Get ready to unleash your creativity!

4.3 Working with Sass Variables and Mixins

Alright, let's take our Bootstrap 5 customization skills to the next level with Sass! If you recall from Section 4.1, Sass is a powerful CSS preprocessor that adds some seriously handy features to your styling workflow. Think of it as CSS with superpowers!

In this section, we'll focus on two key Sass features: variables and mixins. These tools will allow you to customize Bootstrap in a more organized and efficient way, making your styles easier to maintain and update.

Sass Variables: Your Customization Control Panel

Imagine having a control panel where you can adjust the colors, fonts, and spacing of your entire website with just a few clicks. That's essentially what Sass variables offer.

Bootstrap 5 uses Sass variables extensively to define its default styles. These variables are like the settings in your control panel. By modifying them, you can change the look and feel of your entire website without having to edit countless CSS rules individually.

Here's an example:

SCSS

```scss
// Change the primary color to green
$primary: #007bff;
```

This code snippet modifies the $primary variable, which controls the primary color used throughout Bootstrap. By changing this single variable, you can instantly update the color of all primary buttons, links, and other elements that use this variable.

Bootstrap's _variables.scss file contains a vast collection of variables that control various aspects of the framework's styles. You can find this file in the scss folder of the Bootstrap source code.

Sass Mixins: Reusable Style Recipes

Mixins are like reusable code snippets that you can include in your Sass files. They allow you to define a set of styles once and then reuse them throughout your project, saving you time and effort.

Think of mixins as recipes for creating specific styles. You define the ingredients (CSS properties) and instructions (values) once, and then you can use that recipe whenever you need to create that particular style.

Here's an example:

SCSS

```
// Define a mixin for adding a box shadow
@mixin box-shadow($x, $y, $blur, $color) {
  box-shadow: $x $y $blur $color;
}

// Use the mixin to apply a box shadow to a button
.btn-primary {
  @include box-shadow(0, 2px, 5px, rgba(0, 0, 0, 0.2));
}
```

This code defines a mixin called box-shadow that takes four parameters: the x-offset, y-offset, blur radius, and color of the shadow. You can then use this mixin to apply a box shadow to any element, like the .btn-primary class in this example.

Combining Variables and Mixins

You can combine variables and mixins to create even more powerful and flexible customization options.

For example, you could define a mixin that uses a variable to control the background color of an element:

SCSS

```
// Define a variable for the background color
$bg-color: #f8f9fa;

// Define a mixin that uses the variable
@mixin background {
  background-color: $bg-color;
}

// Use the mixin to apply the background color
.my-element {
  @include background;
}
```

This allows you to easily change the background color of multiple elements by simply modifying the $bg-color variable.

Compiling Sass

To use Sass in your project, you'll need to compile it into regular CSS. This is typically done using a command-line tool or a task runner like Gulp or Grunt.

Don't worry if you're not familiar with these tools yet. We'll cover them in more detail in later chapters. For now, you can use online Sass compilers or code editors with built-in Sass compilation features to experiment with Sass variables and mixins.

Illustrating the Power

Imagine you're designing a website with a specific brand color. You can define a Sass variable for that color and use it throughout your stylesheet. If you later decide to change the brand color, you only need to update that single variable, and the change will be reflected across your entire website.

Mixins can help you create consistent styles for common elements, like buttons or cards. You can define a mixin with your desired styles and then reuse it whenever you need to create a new button or card, ensuring consistency and saving time.

Experiment and Explore!

Sass variables and mixins are powerful tools for customizing Bootstrap 5. They allow you to create more maintainable, flexible, and efficient stylesheets.

I encourage you to experiment with these features and explore how they can enhance your Bootstrap workflow.

In the next section, we'll dive deeper into customization by exploring how to create custom themes with Sass.

4.4 Creating Custom Themes

Alright, let's unleash the full power of Sass and create our own custom Bootstrap 5 themes! This is where you can truly let your creativity shine and build websites that stand out from the crowd.

Think of it like this: instead of just altering a suit off the rack, you're designing your own bespoke clothing line. You choose the fabrics, colors, patterns, and cuts to create a unique style that reflects your brand identity.

Similarly, with Sass, you can transform Bootstrap 5 into something entirely your own. You can modify its core variables, create custom components, and build a theme that perfectly matches your vision.

The Theme Building Process

Here's a step-by-step guide to creating custom Bootstrap 5 themes:

1. Start with the Source Files:

- If you haven't already, download the Bootstrap 5 source files from the official website. You'll find them in the scss folder.

2. Create a Custom Sass File:

- In your project folder, create a new file named custom.scss (or any name you prefer). This is where you'll write your custom Sass code.

3. Import Bootstrap's Sass Files:

- At the top of your custom.scss file, import Bootstrap's _variables.scss file. This will give you access to all of Bootstrap's variables.

```
SCSS
@import "bootstrap/scss/variables";
```

4. Override Variables:

- Now, the fun begins! Start overriding Bootstrap's default variables with your own values. You can change colors, fonts, spacing, breakpoints, and much more.

```scss
// Change the primary color
$primary: #00d9a3;

// Change the font family
$font-family-sans-serif: 'Roboto', sans-serif;

// Adjust the container width
$container-max-widths: (
  sm: 540px,
  md: 720px,
  lg: 960px,
  xl: 1140px,
  xxl: 1320px
);
```

5. Import the Rest of Bootstrap:

- After overriding the variables, import the rest of Bootstrap's Sass files. This will ensure that your custom variables are applied throughout the framework.

SCSS

```
@import "bootstrap/scss/bootstrap";
```

6. Compile Your Sass:

- Use a Sass compiler (like the one built into your code editor or a command-line tool) to compile your custom.scss file into a regular CSS file (e.g., custom.css).

7. Link Your Custom CSS:

- In your HTML file, link your custom.css file after the default Bootstrap CSS file. This ensures that your custom styles take precedence.

HTML

```
<link
href="https://cdn.jsdelivr.net/npm/bootstrap@5.3.0/dist/css/bootstra
p.min.css"              rel="stylesheet"              integrity="sha384-
9ndCyUaIbzAi2FUVXJi0CjmCapSmO7SnpJef0486qhLnuZ2cdeRhO02iuK6FUUVM"
crossorigin="anonymous">
<link rel="stylesheet" href="custom.css">
```

Tips for Creating Themes

- **Start with a Plan**: Before you dive into customization, think about the overall look and feel you want to achieve. Create a mood board or style guide to help you stay focused.
- **Organize Your Sass**: Use comments and clear variable names to keep your Sass code organized and easy to understand.
- **Test Thoroughly**: As you make changes, test your theme on different browsers and devices to ensure it looks and functions correctly.
- **Consider Accessibility**: Keep accessibility in mind when customizing colors and fonts. Ensure sufficient contrast and use appropriate font sizes.

Illustrating the Transformation

Imagine you're building a website for a nature-themed company. You might choose earthy green tones for your primary color, a natural-looking font like Open Sans, and wider container widths to create a spacious feel.

By customizing Bootstrap's variables, you can transform the framework's default blue and gray color scheme into a vibrant green palette that perfectly reflects the company's brand identity.

Experiment and Explore!

Creating custom themes is a rewarding way to unleash your creativity and build truly unique websites with Bootstrap 5.

I encourage you to experiment with different variable overrides, explore new color palettes, and create themes that express your individual style.

In the next section, we'll shift our focus to the practical application of Bootstrap 5 by building a complete blog website with a custom theme. Get ready to put your skills to the test!

4.5 Project: Styling a Blog with a Custom Theme

Alright, it's time to put all our customization knowledge into practice and build a stylish blog website with a custom Bootstrap 5 theme! This project will combine everything we've learned so far: grids, components, Sass variables, and mixins.

We'll create a blog with a unique color scheme, custom fonts, and a responsive layout that looks fantastic on all devices. Get ready to unleash your inner designer!

1. Setting Up the Structure

1. Create a new project folder: Create a new folder for your blog project (e.g., "my-blog").
2. Create HTML files: Inside the folder, create two HTML files: index.html (for the blog homepage) and post.html (for individual blog posts).
3. Create a Sass file: Create a new file named custom.scss in your project folder. This is where you'll define your custom theme.

4. Link the files: In both HTML files, link the Bootstrap CSS file and your custom CSS file (which we'll create later by compiling custom.scss).

HTML

```
<link
href="https://cdn.jsdelivr.net/npm/bootstrap@5.3.0/dist/css/bootstra
p.min.css" rel="stylesheet" integrity="sha384-
9ndCyUaIbzAi2FUVXJi0CjmCapSmO7SnpJef0486qhLnuZ2cdeRhO02iuK6FUUVM"
crossorigin="anonymous">
<link rel="stylesheet" href="custom.css">
```

2. Defining the Custom Theme

1. Import Bootstrap variables: In your custom.scss file, import Bootstrap's _variables.scss file.

SCSS

```
@import "bootstrap/scss/variables";
```

2. Override variables: Customize the following variables to create your unique theme:

SCSS

```
// Color palette
$primary: #663399; // Purple
$secondary: #f8f9fa; // Light gray
$body-bg: #ffffff; // White

// Font family
$font-family-sans-serif: 'Open Sans', sans-serif;

// Container width
$container-max-widths: (
  sm: 540px,
  md: 720px,
  lg: 960px,
  xl: 1140px,
  xxl: 1320px
);

// Link styles
$link-color: $primary;
$link-hover-color: darken($primary, 15%);

// Heading styles
$headings-font-weight: 600;

// More customizations...
```

3. Import Bootstrap: Import the rest of Bootstrap's Sass files.

```scss
SCSS

@import "bootstrap/scss/bootstrap";
```

4. Compile Sass: Compile your custom.scss file into custom.css.

3. Building the Blog Homepage (index.html)

1. **Create the header:** Add a navbar with your blog's title and navigation links.

```html
HTML
<nav class="navbar navbar-expand-lg navbar-light bg-light">
  <div class="container">
    <a class="navbar-brand" href="#">My Blog</a>
    <ul class="navbar-nav">
      <li class="nav-item">
        <a class="nav-link active" aria-current="page"
href="#">Home</a>
      </li>
      <li class="nav-item">
        <a class="nav-link" href="#">About</a>
      </li>
```

```
          <li class="nav-item">
            <a class="nav-link" href="#">Contact</a>
          </li>
        </ul>
      </div>
    </nav>
```

2. **Create the main content area**: Use the grid system to create a two-column layout. The left column will contain blog posts, and the right column will be a sidebar.

```
HTML
<div class="container">
  <div class="row">
    <div class="col-md-8">
      </div>
    <div class="col-md-4">
      </div>
  </div>
</div>
```

3. **Add blog posts**: Create card components for each blog post, including a title, image, excerpt, and "Read More" link.

HTML

```
<div class="card mb-4">
  <img src="images/post1.jpg" class="card-img-top" alt="Blog Post 1">
  <div class="card-body">
    <h5 class="card-title">Blog Post Title 1</h5>
    <p class="card-text">This is an excerpt from the blog post...</p>
    <a href="post.html" class="btn btn-primary">Read More</a>
  </div>
</div>
```

4. **Add sidebar content:** Include widgets or other content in the sidebar, such as a search bar, categories list, or recent posts.

4. Building the Blog Post Page (post.html)

1. Create the header: Use the same navbar as the homepage.
2. Display the blog post: Include the full content of the blog post, using headings, paragraphs, images, and other elements as needed.

5. Running the Code

- Save your HTML and CSS files.
- Open index.html in your web browser.

You should see a stylish blog website with your custom theme applied. The layout should be responsive, adapting to different screen sizes.

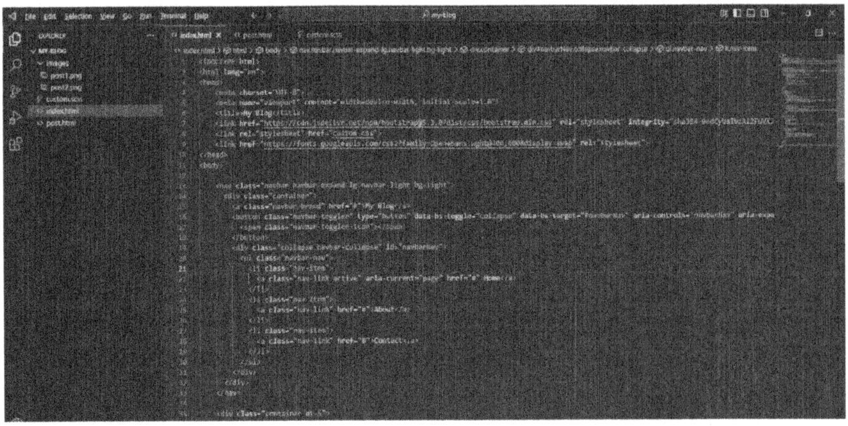

%20Development/my-blog/index.html

Blog Post Title - My Blog
My Blog
Home
Blog Post Title
This is the full content of the blog post. Lorem ipsum dolor sit amet, consectetur adipiscing elit. Maecenas sed diam eget risus varius blandit sit amet non magna. Nullam id dolor id nibh ultricies vehicula ut id elit. Donec ullamcorper nulla non metus auctor fringilla.
Cras mattis consectetur purus sit amet fermentum. Maecenas faucibus mollis interdum. Aenean lacinia bibendum nulla sed consectetur. Donec sed odio dui. Vivamus sagittis lacus vel augue laoreet rutrum faucibus dolor auctor. Donec sed odio dui. Maecenas sed diam eget risus varius blandit sit amet non magna.
Cras mattis consectetur purus sit amet fermentum. Maecenas faucibus mollis interdum. Aenean lacinia bibendum nulla sed consectetur. Donec sed odio dui. Vivamus sagittis lacus vel augue laoreet rutrum faucibus dolor auctor. Donec sed odio dui. Maecenas sed diam eget risus varius blandit sit amet non magna.

Source Code:

HTML

```
<!DOCTYPE html>
<html lang="en">
<head>
    <meta charset="UTF-8">
    <meta name="viewport" content="width=device-width, initial-scale=1.0">
    <title>My Blog</title>
    <link
href="https://cdn.jsdelivr.net/npm/bootstrap@5.3.0/dist/css/bootstrap.min.css
"                    rel="stylesheet"                    integrity="sha384-
9ndCyUaIbzAi2FUVXJi0CjmCapSmO7SnpJef0486qhLnuZ2cdeRhO02iuK6FUUVM"
crossorigin="anonymous">
    <link rel="stylesheet" href="custom.css">
    <link
href="https://fonts.googleapis.com/css2?family=Open+Sans:wght@400;600&display
=swap" rel="stylesheet">
</head>
<body>

    <nav class="navbar navbar-expand-lg navbar-light bg-light">
      <div class="container">
        <a class="navbar-brand" href="#">My Blog</a>
        <button class="navbar-toggler" type="button" data-bs-toggle="collapse"
data-bs-target="#navbarNav"  aria-controls="navbarNav"  aria-expanded="false"
aria-label="Toggle navigation">
```

```
        <span class="navbar-toggler-icon"></span>
      </button>
      <div class="collapse navbar-collapse" id="navbarNav">
        <ul class="navbar-nav">
          <li class="nav-item">
            <a class="nav-link active" aria-current="page" href="#">Home</a>
          </li>
          <li class="nav-item">
            <a class="nav-link" href="#">About</a>
          </li>
          <li class="nav-item">
            <a class="nav-link" href="#">Contact</a>
          </li>
        </ul>
      </div>
    </div>
  </nav>

  <div class="container mt-5">
    <div class="row">
      <div class="col-md-8">

        <div class="card mb-4">
          <img src="images/post1.jpg" class="card-img-top" alt="Blog Post 1">
          <div class="card-body">
            <h5 class="card-title">Blog Post Title 1</h5>
```

```
            <p class="card-text">This is an excerpt from the blog post. Lorem
ipsum dolor sit amet, consectetur adipiscing elit. Maecenas sed diam eget risus
varius blandit sit amet non magna.</p>
            <a href="post.html" class="btn btn-primary">Read More</a>
          </div>
        </div>

        <div class="card mb-4">
          <img src="images/post2.jpg" class="card-img-top" alt="Blog Post 2">
          <div class="card-body">
            <h5 class="card-title">Blog Post Title 2</h5>
            <p class="card-text">Another excerpt from a different blog post.
Nullam id dolor id nibh ultricies vehicula ut id elit. Donec ullamcorper nulla
non metus auctor fringilla.</p>
            <a href="post.html" class="btn btn-primary">Read More</a>
          </div>
        </div>

      </div>
      <div class="col-md-4">

        <div class="card mb-4">
          <div class="card-header">
            About Me
          </div>
          <div class="card-body">
```

```
          <p class="card-text">This is where you can write a short bio about
yourself or your blog.</p>
        </div>
      </div>

      <div class="card mb-4">
        <div class="card-header">
          Categories
        </div>
        <ul class="list-group list-group-flush">
          <li class="list-group-item"><a href="#">Technology</a></li>
          <li class="list-group-item"><a href="#">Design</a></li>
          <li class="list-group-item"><a href="#">Culture</a></li>
        </ul>
      </div>

    </div>
  </div>
</div>

<script
src="https://cdn.jsdelivr.net/npm/bootstrap@5.3.0/dist/js/bootstrap.bundle.mi
n.js"                                    integrity="sha384-
geWF76RCwLtnZ8qwWowPQNguL3RmwHVBC9FhGdlKrxdiJJigb/j/68SIy3Te4Bkz"
crossorigin="anonymous"></script>
</body>
</html>
```

post.html

HTML

```
<!DOCTYPE html>
<html lang="en">
<head>
    <meta charset="UTF-8">
    <meta name="viewport" content="width=device-width, initial-scale=1.0">
    <title>Blog Post Title - My Blog</title>
    <link
href="https://cdn.jsdelivr.net/npm/bootstrap@5.3.0/dist/css/bootstrap.min.css
"                    rel="stylesheet"                    integrity="sha384-
9ndCyUaIbzAi2FUVXJi0CjmCapSmO7SnpJef0486qhLnuZ2cdeRhO02iuK6FUUVM"
crossorigin="anonymous">
    <link rel="stylesheet" href="custom.css">
    <link
href="https://fonts.googleapis.com/css2?family=Open+Sans:wght@400;600&display
=swap" rel="stylesheet">
</head>
<body>

    <nav class="navbar navbar-expand-lg navbar-light bg-light">
      <div class="container">
        <a class="navbar-brand" href="#">My Blog</a>
        <button class="navbar-toggler" type="button" data-bs-toggle="collapse"
data-bs-target="#navbarNav"  aria-controls="navbarNav"  aria-expanded="false"
aria-label="Toggle navigation">
          <span class="navbar-toggler-icon"></span>
```

```
        </button>
        <div class="collapse navbar-collapse" id="navbarNav">
          <ul class="navbar-nav">
            <li class="nav-item">
              <a class="nav-link active" aria-current="page" href="#">Home</a>
            </li>
            <li class="nav-item">
              <a class="nav-link" href="#">About</a>
            </li>
            <li class="nav-item">
              <a class="nav-link" href="#">Contact</a>
            </li>
          </ul>
        </div>
      </div>
    </nav>
    <div class="container mt-5">
      <div class="row">
        <div class="col-md-8">
          <article>
            <h1 class="mb-4">Blog Post Title</h1>
            <img src="images/post1.jpg" class="img-fluid mb-4" alt="Blog Post
Image">
            <p>This is the full content of the blog post. Lorem ipsum dolor sit
amet, consectetur adipiscing elit. Maecenas sed diam eget risus varius blandit
sit amet non magna. Nullam id dolor id nibh ultricies vehicula ut id elit. Donec
ullamcorper nulla non metus auctor fringilla.</p>
```

```
            <p>Cras mattis consectetur purus sit amet fermentum. Maecenas faucibus mollis interdum. Aenean lacinia bibendum nulla sed consectetur. Donec sed odio dui. Vivamus sagittis lacus vel augue laoreet rutrum faucibus dolor auctor. Donec sed odio dui. Maecenas sed diam eget risus varius blandit sit amet non magna.</p>
            <p>Cras mattis consectetur purus sit amet fermentum. Maecenas faucibus mollis interdum. Aenean lacinia bibendum nulla sed consectetur. Donec sed odio dui. Vivamus sagittis lacus vel augue laoreet rutrum faucibus dolor auctor. Donec sed odio dui. Maecenas sed diam eget risus varius blandit sit amet non magna.</p>
          </article>
        </div>
        <div class="col-md-4">
          </div>
      </div>
    </div>
    <script src="https://cdn.jsdelivr.net/npm/bootstrap@5.3.0/dist/js/bootstrap.bundle.min.js" integrity="sha384-geWF76RCwLtnZ8qwWowPQNguL3RmwHVBC9FhGdlKrxdiJJigb/j/68SIy3Te4Bkz" crossorigin="anonymous"></script>
</body>
</html>
```

custom.scss

SCSS

```scss
@import "bootstrap/scss/variables";

// Color palette

$primary: #663399; // Purple

$secondary: #f8f9fa; // Light gray

$body-bg: #ffffff; // White

// Font family

$font-family-sans-serif: 'Open Sans', sans-serif;

// Container width

$container-max-widths: (

  sm: 540px,

  md: 720px,

  lg: 960px,

  xl: 1140px,

  xxl: 1320px

);

// Link styles

$link-color: $primary;

$link-hover-color: darken($primary, 15%);

// Heading styles

$headings-font-weight: 600;

// More customizations...
@import "bootstrap/scss/bootstrap";
```

Remember to:

- Replace "images/post1.jpg" and "images/post2.jpg" with the actual paths to your image files.
- Compile the custom.scss file into a custom.css file using a Sass compiler.
- Make sure the paths to the CSS and JavaScript files are correct in your HTML files.
- Add more blog posts and sidebar content as needed.

Illustrating the Interface:

Imagine a visually appealing blog with a purple color scheme and a clean, modern font. The homepage features a navbar with the blog's title and navigation links. Below the navbar, the page is divided into two columns. The left column displays a series of blog posts, each presented as a card with an image, title, excerpt, and "Read More" link. The right column contains a sidebar with widgets or other content.

The blog post page displays the full content of the post with a clear and readable layout.

Congratulations! You've just built a stylish blog website with a custom Bootstrap 5 theme. This project demonstrates how to combine grids, components, and Sass customization to create a unique and responsive website.

Keep experimenting with different layouts, content, and styles to further enhance your Bootstrap skills and build even more impressive websites.

Part II: Building Engaging User Interfaces

CHAPTER 5:
CRAFTING DYNAMIC HOMEPAGES

5.1 Homepage Design Principles

Alright, let's shift gears and talk about homepages! As the digital front door to your website, your homepage plays a crucial role in making a strong first impression and guiding visitors toward their goals.

Think of it like this: your homepage is the lobby of your online business. It needs to be welcoming, informative, and easy to navigate. You want visitors to feel immediately at ease and understand what your website is all about within seconds.

Crafting a dynamic homepage that captivates visitors and drives conversions requires a thoughtful blend of design principles, user experience considerations, and a touch of creative flair. Let's explore some key principles to keep in mind as we embark on this journey.

1. Clarity and Purpose

First and foremost, your homepage needs to be crystal clear about its purpose. What is the main message you want to convey? What actions do you want visitors to take?

Think of it like a newspaper headline: It needs to grab attention and communicate the essence of the story in just a few words.

Here are some questions to consider:

- What is the primary goal of your website? (e.g., selling products, providing information, building a community)
- Who is your target audience? (e.g., tech-savvy millennials, busy professionals, curious students)
- What are the key actions you want visitors to take? (e.g., sign up for a newsletter, browse products, learn more about your services)

Once you have a clear understanding of your homepage's purpose, you can structure your content and design elements to support those goals.

2. Visual Hierarchy

Our eyes naturally gravitate towards certain elements on a page. By using visual hierarchy effectively, you can guide visitors' attention to the most important information.

Think of it like a well-designed magazine layout: Headings, images, and calls to action are strategically placed to draw the eye and create a visual flow.

Here are some techniques to establish visual hierarchy:

- Size: Use larger font sizes for headings and important elements.
- Color: Use contrasting colors to highlight key information.
- Spacing: Use white space to create visual breathing room and separate different sections.
- Position: Place the most important content above the fold (the area visible without scrolling).

3. User Experience (UX)

A dynamic homepage is not just about aesthetics; it's about creating a positive user experience. Visitors should be able to easily find what they're looking for and navigate the site effortlessly.

Think of it like a well-organized store: Products are logically categorized, signage is clear, and the checkout process is smooth.

Here are some UX considerations:

- Navigation: Make sure your navigation menu is clear, concise, and easy to use.
- Search: Provide a prominent search bar for users who know what they're looking for.
- Content: Keep your content concise, engaging, and relevant to your target audience.
- Call to action: Use clear and compelling calls to action to guide users towards desired actions.
- Mobile-friendliness: Ensure your homepage is responsive and looks great on all devices.

4. Engaging Content

Your homepage content should be more than just a wall of text. Use a variety of elements to keep visitors engaged and interested.

Think of it like a captivating story: It has a beginning, middle, and end, with compelling characters and a clear narrative.

Here are some content ideas:

- Headline: A strong headline that grabs attention and communicates your main message.
- Subheading: A brief explanation of what you offer or what makes you unique.
- Images and videos: Visuals that capture attention and convey your brand personality.
- Testimonials: Social proof that builds trust and credibility.
- Call to action: A clear and compelling call to action that encourages visitors to take the next step.

5. Branding and Consistency

Your homepage should be consistent with your overall brand identity. Use your brand colors, fonts, and imagery to create a cohesive look and feel.

Think of it like a well-dressed person: Their clothes, accessories, and overall style work together to create a polished and professional image.

Here are some branding considerations:

- Logo: Prominently display your logo in the header.
- Color scheme: Use your brand colors throughout the page.
- Typography: Use consistent fonts that reflect your brand personality.
- Imagery: Choose images that align with your brand values and messaging.

6. Performance

A slow-loading homepage can be a major turn-off for visitors. Optimize your images, minimize HTTP requests, and use caching to ensure your page loads quickly.

Think of it like a fast-paced movie: You don't want any lag or buffering that interrupts the flow and loses the viewer's attention.

Illustrating the Principles

Imagine a homepage with a clear headline that immediately tells you what the website is about. The most important information is prominently displayed above the fold, and the navigation menu is easy to use. The page uses a visually appealing color scheme and high-quality images. The content is concise and engaging, and there are clear calls to action throughout.

This homepage effectively incorporates the key design principles we've discussed, creating a positive user experience and encouraging visitors to explore further.

Experiment and Explore!

Designing dynamic homepages is an iterative process. Experiment with different layouts, content, and styles to see what works best for your website and your target audience.

In the next section, we'll put these principles into practice and build a homepage for our fictional "Hush" noise-canceling app. Get ready to unleash your creativity!

5.2 Building Hero Sections with Impact

Alright, let's talk about hero sections! These prominent areas, typically found at the top of a homepage, are your chance to make a bold first impression and capture your visitors' attention. Think of them as the movie trailers of your website – they need to be captivating, informative, and leave people wanting more.

Building a hero section that truly packs a punch requires a thoughtful combination of design elements, compelling content, and a clear call to action. Let's break down the key ingredients:

1. Visuals that Wow

The hero section is often the first visual element visitors encounter, so it needs to be visually striking. High-quality images or videos that are relevant to your brand and message can instantly grab attention and set the tone for your website.

Think of it like a billboard: It needs to be eye-catching and memorable, even at a glance.

Here are some visual considerations:

- **High-resolution images:** Use crisp, professional images that are optimized for web use.
- **Video backgrounds:** A well-produced video can create a truly immersive experience.
- **Graphics and illustrations:** Custom graphics or illustrations can add a unique touch.
- **Color scheme:** Choose colors that align with your brand and evoke the desired emotions.

2. Compelling Content

Once you've captured attention with visuals, you need to follow up with compelling content that clearly communicates your message and value proposition.

Think of it like an elevator pitch: You need to convey the essence of what you offer in a concise and engaging way.

Here are some content elements to consider:

- Headline: A strong, concise headline that grabs attention and communicates your main message.

- Subheading: A brief explanation of what you offer or what makes you unique.
- Call to action: A clear and prominent call to action that encourages visitors to take the next step.

3. Clear Call to Action

A hero section without a clear call to action is like a movie trailer without a release date. You need to tell visitors what you want them to do next.

Think of it like a road sign: It needs to point visitors in the right direction.

Here are some examples of effective calls to action:

- "Sign up now"
- "Learn more"
- "Get started"
- "Shop now"
- "Download the app"

Make sure your call to action is visually prominent and uses action-oriented language.

4. Responsive Design

Your hero section should look great on all devices, from smartphones to large desktops. Use Bootstrap's grid system and responsive utilities to ensure your content adapts seamlessly to different screen sizes.

Think of it like a chameleon: It needs to blend in and look its best in any environment.

5. Accessibility

Make sure your hero section is accessible to everyone, including people with disabilities. Use sufficient color contrast, provide alternative text for images, and ensure your content is easily navigable with assistive technologies.

Think of it like a universal design: It needs to be usable by everyone, regardless of their abilities.

Building a Hero Section with Bootstrap 5

Let's put these principles into practice and build a hero section for our "Hush" noise-canceling app using Bootstrap 5:

HTML

```
<div class="container-fluid p-0">
  <div class="jumbotron jumbotron-fluid bg-cover text-white" style="background-image: url('images/hero-image.jpg');">
    <div class="container">
      <h1 class="display-4">Find Your Focus with Hush</h1>
      <p class="lead">Escape the noise and boost your productivity with our revolutionary noise-canceling app.</p>
      <a href="#" class="btn btn-primary btn-lg">Download Now</a>
    </div>
  </div>
</div>
```

In this code:

- container-fluid p-0 creates a full-width container with no padding.
- jumbotron jumbotron-fluid bg-cover text-white creates a large hero section with a background image, full-width content, and white text.
- style="background-image: url('images/hero-image.jpg');" sets the background image (replace with your actual image path).
- display-4 and lead classes are used for the heading and subheading.

- btn btn-primary btn-lg creates a prominent call-to-action button.

Illustrating the Interface:

Imagine a captivating hero section with a stunning background image of someone peacefully working in a bustling coffee shop. The headline "Find Your Focus with Hush" is prominently displayed in large, white text. Below the headline, a concise subheading explains the app's benefits. A bright blue "Download Now" button encourages visitors to take action.

This hero section effectively combines visuals, compelling content, and a clear call to action to create a powerful first impression.

Experiment and Explore!

Building impactful hero sections is an art. Experiment with different layouts, visuals, and content to see what works best for your website and your brand.

In the next section, we'll explore how to showcase your product's features and benefits effectively on your homepage.

5.3 Showcasing Features and Benefits

Alright, you've hooked your visitors with a killer hero section. Now it's time to reel them in by showcasing what your product or service has to offer! This is where you highlight the key features and benefits that make you stand out from the crowd.

Think of it like this: you're giving a presentation about a new invention. You wouldn't just say, "Here it is!" You'd explain what it does, how it works, and why people should be excited about it.

Similarly, when showcasing features and benefits on your homepage, you need to go beyond simply listing them. You need to present them in a way that's engaging, informative, and persuasive.

1. Focus on Benefits, Not Just Features

While features are important, they're only valuable if they translate into tangible benefits for the user.

Think of it like this: A car might have a powerful engine (feature), but what really matters to the buyer is that it allows them to accelerate quickly and overtake with confidence (benefit).

Here's how to focus on benefits:

- **For each feature, ask "So what?"** What does this feature enable the user to do or achieve?
- **Use customer-centric language**: Focus on how the features improve the user's life or solve their problems.
- **Quantify benefits whenever possible**: Use data, statistics, or testimonials to support your claims.

2. Use Visuals to Enhance Understanding

Visuals can be incredibly powerful in conveying information and making your features and benefits more tangible.

Think of it like a product demonstration: Seeing the product in action is much more compelling than just hearing about it.

Here are some visual options:

- Images: Show your product in use or highlight key features with close-up shots.

- Videos: Create short explainer videos or product demos.
- Infographics: Present data and statistics in a visually engaging way.
- Icons: Use icons to represent features or benefits visually.

3. Structure for Clarity

Organize your features and benefits in a clear and logical way. Use headings, subheadings, and bullet points to break up the text and make it easier to scan.

Think of it like a well-organized presentation: Each slide has a clear purpose and builds upon the previous one.

Here are some structural options:

- **Feature grids**: Present features and benefits in a grid layout with visuals and concise descriptions.
- **Tabbed content**: Use tabs to organize features into different categories.
- **Accordion sections**: Allow users to expand and collapse sections to reveal more details.

4. Keep it Concise

No one wants to read a wall of text on a homepage. Keep your descriptions concise and to the point, focusing on the most important information.

Think of it like a tweet: You need to convey your message in a limited number of characters.

5. Use a Strong Call to Action

Don't forget to include a clear call to action at the end of your features and benefits section. Encourage visitors to learn more, sign up, or make a purchase.

Think of it like the climax of a movie: It's the moment where the audience is most engaged and ready to take action.

Showcasing Hush's Features

Let's apply these principles to our "Hush" noise-canceling app:

HTML

```
<div class="container">
  <div class="row">
    <div class="col-md-4">
```

```
        <img src="images/feature1.jpg" alt="Personalized Soundscapes" class="img-fluid mb-4">
        <h2>Personalized Soundscapes</h2>
        <p>Create your perfect audio environment with customizable soundscapes and ambient noises. Block out distractions and boost your focus with personalized sounds that work for you.</p>
      </div>
      <div class="col-md-4">
        <img src="images/feature2.jpg" alt="AI-Powered Noise Cancellation" class="img-fluid mb-4">
        <h2>AI-Powered Noise Cancellation</h2>
        <p>Our advanced AI algorithms intelligently filter out distractions, leaving you in peace. Whether you're in a busy coffee shop or a noisy office, Hush will help you find your quiet place.</p>
      </div>
      <div class="col-md-4">
        <img src="images/feature3.jpg" alt="Focus Modes" class="img-fluid mb-4">
        <h2>Focus Modes</h2>
        <p>Choose from a variety of focus modes designed to optimize your concentration and productivity. Whether you need to block out all distractions or just reduce background noise, Hush has a mode for you.</p>
      </div>
    </div>
    <div class="row mt-5">
      <div class="col-md-12 text-center">
```

```
        <a href="#" class="btn btn-primary btn-lg">Try Hush for
Free</a>
      </div>
    </div>
</div>
```

In this code:

- We use a three-column grid to showcase three key features.
- Each column includes an image, a heading, and a concise description that highlights the benefit of the feature.
- A centered call to action encourages visitors to try the app.

Illustrating the Interface:

Imagine a section with three visually appealing columns. Each column showcases a different feature of the Hush app with an image and a concise description. For example, one column might show an image of someone relaxing in a park with headphones on, with the heading "Personalized Soundscapes" and a description of how the app allows users to create their ideal audio environment. At the bottom of the section, a prominent "Try Hush for Free" button encourages visitors to take action.

This section effectively showcases the app's features and benefits in a clear, concise, and visually engaging way.

5.4 Creating Effective Calls to Action

Alright, we've talked about grabbing attention with hero sections and showcasing features and benefits. Now, let's talk about the final piece of the puzzle: creating effective calls to action (CTAs) that drive conversions.

Think of your CTAs as the guiding hand that leads visitors towards your desired outcome. They're the signposts that point them in the right direction, whether it's signing up for a newsletter, making a purchase, or learning more about your services.

Crafting compelling CTAs that inspire action requires a bit of finesse. Here's how to make your CTAs truly effective:

1. Use Action-Oriented Language

Your CTAs should use verbs that inspire action. Instead of passive phrases like "Learn more," use stronger verbs like "Discover," "Explore," or "Get started."

Think of it like a personal trainer: They don't say, "Maybe you could try doing a push-up." They say, "Let's go! Give me 10 push-ups!"

Here are some examples of action-oriented verbs:

- Get
- Download
- Try
- Start
- Join
- Shop
- Discover
- Explore
- Learn

2. Create a Sense of Urgency

Adding a sense of urgency can encourage visitors to take action sooner rather than later.

Think of it like a limited-time offer: It motivates people to act quickly before they miss out.

Here are some ways to create urgency:

- Limited-time offers: "Get 20% off for a limited time only!"
- Scarcity: "Only a few spots left!"
- Time-sensitive language: "Don't miss out!" or "Act now!"

3. Highlight the Value Proposition

Clearly communicate the value visitors will receive by taking action. What's in it for them?

Think of it like a sales pitch: You need to convince people that your product or service is worth their time and money.

Here are some ways to highlight value:

- Offer a free trial or demo.
- Provide a discount or bonus.
- Emphasize the benefits of your product or service.

4. Make Your CTAs Visually Prominent

Your CTAs should stand out on the page. Use contrasting colors, larger font sizes, and whitespace to make them easily noticeable.

Think of it like a big, red "BUY NOW" button: It's hard to miss!

Here are some visual techniques:

- Use contrasting colors: Make your CTA button a different color than the background.
- Use whitespace: Give your CTA button plenty of space around it so it doesn't get lost in the clutter.
- Use larger font sizes: Make the text on your CTA button large and easy to read.

5. Test and Optimize

The best way to find out what works is to test different variations of your CTAs. Try different colors, wording, and placements to see what drives the most conversions.

Think of it like a science experiment: You need to test different variables to find the optimal solution.

Here are some tools for A/B testing:

- Google Optimize: A free tool that allows you to run A/B tests on your website.
- Optimizely: A paid tool with more advanced features for A/B testing and personalization.

Effective CTAs for Hush

Let's create some effective CTAs for our "Hush" noise-canceling app:

- **"Try Hush for Free"** (Highlights the free trial)
- **"Download Now and Start Focusing"** (Action-oriented and emphasizes the benefit)
- **"Limited Time Offer**: Get 50% Off Hush!" (Creates urgency and offers a discount)
- **"Join the Hush Community and Find Your Quiet Place"** (Appeals to the desire for community)

Illustrating Effective CTAs

Imagine a homepage with a prominent "Download Now" button in a contrasting color. The button is placed above the fold and surrounded by whitespace, making it easily noticeable. The button text is large and clear, and it uses action-oriented language.

This CTA is likely to be effective because it's visually prominent, uses strong language, and clearly communicates the next step.

Experiment and Explore!

Creating effective calls to action is an ongoing process. Continuously test and optimize your CTAs to ensure they're driving the desired results.

In the next section, we'll explore how to design and build dynamic homepages for startups.

5.5 Project: Designing a Modern Homepage for a Startup

Let's put our knowledge of homepage design principles into action by creating a modern and engaging homepage for a fictional startup called "ZenHub," a productivity app designed to help users focus and reduce distractions.

1. Define the Core Message:

- **Headline**: Your Zen Zone, Anywhere
- **Subheading**: Boost your focus and productivity with Hush, the ultimate noise-canceling app.
- **Call to Action**: Download Now

2. Choose a Visual Style:

- **Color Palette**: A calming color palette of blues and greens to evoke a sense of tranquility.
- **Typography**: A clean and modern font like Montserrat or Roboto.
- **Imagery**: High-quality images of people working productively in serene environments.

3. Structure the Layout:

- **Hero Section**: A full-width hero section with a large background image and a prominent headline, subheading, and call to action.
- **Feature Section**: A section showcasing the app's key features with icons and concise descriptions.
- **Testimonial Section**: A section featuring testimonials from satisfied users.
- **Footer**: A footer with navigation links, copyright information, and social media links.

4. Implement the Design:

Here's a basic HTML structure for the homepage:

HTML

```
<!DOCTYPE html>
<html lang="en">
<head>
  <meta charset="UTF-8">
  <meta name="viewport" content="width=device-width, initial-
scale=1.0">
  <title>ZenHub</title>
```

```
  <link
href="https://cdn.jsdelivr.net/npm/bootstrap@5.3.0/dist/css/bootstra
p.min.css" rel="stylesheet" integrity="sha384-
9ndCyUaIbzAi2FUVXJi0CjmCapSmO7SnpJef0486qhLnuZ2cdeRhO02iuK6FUUVM"
crossorigin="anonymous">
  <link rel="stylesheet" href="styles.css">
</head>
<body>

  <section class="hero">
    <div class="container">
      <div class="row align-items-center">
        <div class="col-md-6">
          <h1>Your Zen Zone, Anywhere</h1>
          <p>Boost your focus and productivity with Hush, the
ultimate noise-canceling app.</p>
          <a href="#" class="btn btn-primary">Download Now</a>
        </div>
        <div class="col-md-6">
          <img src="images/hero-image.jpg" alt="Person working
peacefully with headphones" class="img-fluid">
        </div>
      </div>
    </div>
  </section>

  <section class="features">
```

```
    <div class="container">
      <div class="row">
        <div class="col-md-4">
          <i class="bi bi-headphones"></i>
          <h3>Noise Cancellation</h3>
          <p>Block out distractions and focus on what matters.</p>
        </div>
        <div class="col-md-4">
          <i class="bi bi-clock"></i>
          <h3>Time Management</h3>
          <p>Set timers and track your focus time to boost
productivity.</p>
        </div>
        <div class="col-md-4">
          <i class="bi bi-heart"></i>
          <h3>Mindful Moments</h3>
          <p>Take breaks and practice mindfulness with guided
meditation.</p>
        </div>
      </div>
    </div>
  </section>

  <section class="testimonials">
    <div class="container">
      <div class="row">
        <div class="col-md-12">
```

```
          <h2>What Our Users Say</h2>
          <div class="testimonial">
            <p>"Hush has been a game-changer for my productivity. I 
can finally focus on my work without distractions."</p>
            <p>- John Doe, Satisfied User</p>
          </div>
          <div class="testimonial">
            <p>"I love the personalized soundscapes. They help me 
relax and unwind after a long day."</p>
            <p>- Jane Smith, Happy User</p>
          </div>
        </div>
      </div>
    </div>
  </section>

  <footer class="footer">
    <div class="container">
      <p>&copy; 2023 ZenHub. All rights reserved.</p>
    </div>
  </footer>

  <script
src="https://cdn.jsdelivr.net/npm/bootstrap@5.3.0/dist/js/bootstrap.
bundle.min.js" integrity="sha384-
geWF76RCwLtnZ8qwWowPQNguL3RmwHVBC9FhGdlKrxdiJJigb/j/68SIy3Te4Bkz"
crossorigin="anonymous"></script>
```

```
</body>
</html>
```

Remember to:

- Replace the placeholder image images/hero-image.jpg with your actual hero image.
- Customize the colors, fonts, and layout to match your brand.
- Add more features, testimonials, and calls to action as needed.
- Optimize your images for web use to improve loading times.
- Consider using a CSS framework like Bootstrap to speed up development and ensure responsiveness.

By following these guidelines and leveraging Bootstrap's powerful components, you can create stunning and engaging homepages that captivate your audience and drive conversions.

CHAPTER 6: DEVELOPING INTERACTIVE DASHBOARDS

6.1 Dashboard Design Best Practices

Alright, let's dive into the world of dashboards! These powerful tools provide a centralized view of key information, helping users monitor data, track progress, and make informed decisions. Think of a dashboard like the cockpit of an airplane – it displays all the essential information the pilot needs to navigate and control the aircraft.

Designing effective dashboards that are both informative and user-friendly requires a thoughtful approach. Here are some best practices to keep in mind:

1. Know Your Audience and Purpose

Before you start designing your dashboard, clearly define:

- **Who will be using it?** What are their roles, responsibilities, and information needs?

- **What is the main purpose of the dashboard?** What key metrics or insights should it convey?

For example, a marketing dashboard might focus on website traffic, conversion rates, and social media engagement, while a sales dashboard might track leads, opportunities, and revenue.

2. Prioritize Clarity and Simplicity

A cluttered dashboard is an ineffective dashboard. Prioritize the most important information and avoid overwhelming users with too much data.

Think of it like a minimalist's apartment: Everything has its place, and there's no unnecessary clutter.

Here's how to achieve clarity:

- **Use clear and concise labels**: Avoid jargon or technical terms that users might not understand.
- **Choose appropriate visualizations**: Use charts and graphs that effectively represent the data.

- **Group related information**: Organize data into logical sections or categories.
- **Use whitespace effectively**: Give elements room to breathe and avoid a cramped layout.

3. Focus on Key Performance Indicators (KPIs)

KPIs are the most important metrics that measure progress towards your goals. Make sure your dashboard prominently displays these KPIs and uses visual cues to highlight their performance.

Think of it like a scoreboard: It clearly shows who's winning and losing.

Here's how to highlight KPIs:

- **Use large, bold fonts**: Make KPIs stand out visually.
- **Use color coding**: Use green to indicate good performance, red for poor performance, and yellow for neutral.
- **Use gauges or charts**: Visually represent KPI progress towards targets.

4. Make it Interactive

Allow users to interact with the dashboard to explore data in more detail. This could include:

- **Filtering data**: Allow users to filter data by date range, category, or other criteria.
- **Drilling down into details**: Enable users to click on charts or graphs to see more detailed information.
- **Customizing views**: Allow users to personalize the dashboard to display the information that's most relevant to them.

Think of it like a control panel: Users should be able to adjust settings and explore different options.

5. Ensure Responsiveness

Your dashboard should look great and function smoothly on all devices, from desktops to mobile phones. Use Bootstrap's grid system and responsive utilities to create a flexible layout that adapts to different screen sizes.

Think of it like a website: It needs to be accessible and user-friendly on any device.

6. Test and Iterate

Get feedback from users and continuously iterate on your dashboard design. What works well? What could be improved?

Think of it like a prototype: You need to test it out and refine it based on user feedback.

Illustrating the Best Practices

Imagine a dashboard with a clean and uncluttered layout. The most important KPIs are displayed prominently at the top, using large fonts and color coding to indicate performance. Charts and graphs are used effectively to visualize data, and users can interact with the dashboard to filter data and drill down into details. The dashboard is responsive and looks great on all devices.

This dashboard effectively incorporates the best practices we've discussed, creating a user-friendly and informative tool that helps users monitor data and make informed decisions.

In the next section, we'll put these best practices into action and build an interactive dashboard with Bootstrap 5.

6.2 Data Visualization with Charts and Graphs

Alright, let's talk about bringing your dashboards to life with data visualization! Charts and graphs are the visual storytellers of your data, transforming raw numbers into meaningful insights that are easy to understand and interpret. Think of them as the illustrations in a children's book – they make the story more engaging and memorable.

Choosing the right chart or graph for your data is crucial. It's like selecting the right tool for the job – a hammer is great for nails, but not so much for screws. Here's a breakdown of some common chart types and when to use them:

1. Line Charts

Line charts are perfect for showing trends over time. They connect data points with lines, making it easy to see how values change over a period.

Think of it like a stock market graph: It shows how a stock's price has fluctuated over days, weeks, or months.

Use line charts for:

- Tracking website traffic over time
- Monitoring sales performance
- Visualizing stock prices
- Showing temperature changes

2. Bar Charts

Bar charts are great for comparing different categories or groups of data. They use bars of varying lengths to represent values, making it easy to see comparisons.

Think of it like a popularity contest: Each bar represents a candidate, and the length of the bar shows how many votes they received.

Use bar charts for:

- Comparing sales figures for different products
- Showing website traffic by source (e.g., organic search, social media)
- Visualizing survey results
- Comparing the performance of different teams

3. Pie Charts

Pie charts are ideal for showing proportions or percentages of a whole. They divide a circle into slices, with each slice representing a different category.

Think of it like a pizza: Each slice represents a different topping, and the size of the slice shows how much of the pizza is covered by that topping.

Use pie charts for:

- Showing market share
- Visualizing budget allocation
- Displaying survey responses with a limited number of options
- Representing the composition of a team or group

4. Scatter Plots

Scatter plots are useful for showing the relationship between two variables. They plot data points on a graph, with each point representing a pair of values.

Think of it like a map of stars: Each star represents a data point, and its position on the map shows its relationship to other stars.

Use scatter plots for:

- Analyzing correlations between variables
- Identifying outliers or trends
- Visualizing data with a large number of data points

5. Other Chart Types

There are many other chart types available, each with its own strengths and weaknesses. Some examples include:

- **Area charts**: Similar to line charts, but the area under the line is filled in.
- **Heatmaps**: Use color to represent values in a grid.
- **Treemaps**: Display hierarchical data as nested rectangles.
- **Gauges**: Visualize a single value in relation to a target or range.

Choosing the Right Chart

The best chart type for your data depends on the specific information you want to convey and the type of data you have. Consider the following factors:

- Type of data: Is it categorical, numerical, or time-series data?
- Purpose of visualization: Are you comparing values, showing trends, or displaying proportions?
- Audience: Who will be viewing the chart? What is their level of data literacy?

Tools for Creating Charts

There are many tools available for creating charts and graphs. Some popular options include:

- **Chart.js**: A JavaScript library for creating interactive charts.
- **D3.js**: A powerful JavaScript library for creating custom data visualizations.
- **Google Charts**: A free service that provides a wide variety of chart types.

- **Excel**: A spreadsheet program that includes basic charting capabilities.

Illustrating Data Visualization

Imagine a dashboard that displays website traffic data. A line chart shows the trend of website visits over time, while a bar chart compares traffic from different sources (e.g., organic search, social media). A pie chart shows the proportion of visitors from different countries.

This dashboard effectively uses different chart types to visualize various aspects of the data, providing a comprehensive and engaging overview of website traffic.

Experiment and Explore!

Data visualization is a powerful tool for communicating insights and making data more meaningful. Experiment with different chart types and tools to find the best way to visualize your data and bring your dashboards to life.

In the next section, we'll explore how to add user input and controls to your dashboards to make them more interactive and dynamic.

6.3 User Input and Controls

Alright, let's make our dashboards truly dynamic by adding user input and controls! This is where we empower users to interact with the data, explore different perspectives, and personalize their experience. Think of it like giving them the steering wheel – they can now choose their own path and explore the data landscape at their own pace.

Adding user input and controls to your dashboards can significantly enhance their usefulness and engagement. Here's how to do it effectively:

1. Filters: Narrowing Down the View

Filters are like the zoom function on a map – they allow users to focus on specific areas of the data. By providing various filter options, you enable users to slice and dice the data to uncover the insights that are most relevant to them.

Think of it like an online store: Users can filter products by category, price range, size, color, and other criteria to find exactly what they're looking for.

Here are some common filter types:

- Date range: Allow users to select a specific time period to analyze data within that range.
- Category: Enable users to filter data by different categories or groups.
- Value: Allow users to filter data based on specific values or ranges.
- Search: Provide a search bar to filter data based on keywords or phrases.

2. Drill-Downs: Exploring the Details

Drill-downs are like clicking on a link to learn more – they allow users to delve deeper into the data and explore specific details. By providing drill-down capabilities, you enable users to uncover hidden patterns and insights that might not be immediately apparent at a high level.

Think of it like an investigative report: Start with a broad overview, then drill down into specific details to uncover the full story.

Here's how to implement drill-downs:

- Clickable charts and graphs: Allow users to click on specific data points or sections of a chart to see more detailed information.
- Interactive tables: Enable users to click on rows or columns to expand and see more data.
- Linked dashboards: Create separate dashboards that focus on specific areas of the data and link them together for seamless navigation.

3. Customizable Views: Personalizing the Experience

Allowing users to customize their dashboard view is like letting them rearrange the furniture in their living room – it gives them a sense of ownership and control over their environment. By providing customization options, you empower users to create a dashboard that perfectly suits their individual needs and preferences.

Think of it like a personalized news feed: Users can choose the topics they're interested in and customize the layout to their liking.

Here are some customization options:

- Rearranging widgets: Allow users to drag and drop widgets to change their position on the dashboard.
- Adding or removing widgets: Enable users to add or remove widgets based on their needs.
- Changing chart types: Allow users to switch between different chart types to visualize data in different ways.
- Saving layouts: Enable users to save their customized layouts for future use.

4. Input Fields: Adding New Data

Input fields allow users to add new data to the dashboard, making it a truly interactive and collaborative tool.

Think of it like a spreadsheet: Users can enter new data, edit existing data, and update the dashboard in real-time.

Here are some examples of input fields:

- Text fields: For entering text or numerical data.
- Date pickers: For selecting dates or date ranges.
- Dropdown menus: For selecting from a list of options.

- Checkboxes and radio buttons: For making choices or selections.

5. Implementing User Input with Bootstrap 5

Bootstrap 5 provides a variety of components that can be used to implement user input and controls in your dashboards.

- **Forms**: Use Bootstrap's form controls (input fields, buttons, checkboxes, etc.) to create filters, drill-downs, and input forms.
- **Dropdowns**: Use Bootstrap's dropdown component to create filter menus or navigation options.
- **Modals**: Use Bootstrap's modal component to display detailed information or forms in a pop-up window.
- **JavaScript**: Use JavaScript to handle user interactions and update the dashboard dynamically.

Illustrating User Input and Controls

Imagine a dashboard that displays sales data. Users can filter the data by date range, product category, and sales region. They can click on a bar chart to drill down into specific sales figures for a particular product. They can also customize the dashboard by rearranging widgets and adding new charts.

This dashboard effectively incorporates user input and controls, making it a powerful tool for exploring and analyzing sales data.

Experiment and Explore!

Adding user input and controls can significantly enhance the functionality and engagement of your dashboards. Experiment with different options and find the best way to empower your users to interact with the data and personalize their experience.

In the next section, we'll explore how to create dynamic and responsive dashboards that adapt to different screen sizes and devices.

6.4 Creating Dynamic and Responsive Dashboards

Okay, we've covered the essentials of dashboard design and data visualization. Now, let's combine those skills with our Bootstrap 5 expertise to create dashboards that are both dynamic and responsive!

Think of it like building a transformer – your dashboard needs to adapt and morph seamlessly to fit different screen sizes and devices, while still providing a rich and interactive experience.

Here's how to achieve this:

1. Embrace the Bootstrap Grid

Bootstrap's grid system is your best friend when it comes to building responsive layouts. Use rows and columns to structure your dashboard elements, and leverage breakpoint prefixes (-sm, -md, -lg, etc.) to control how they behave on different screen sizes.

Think of it like a puzzle: Arrange the pieces (widgets) on the board (grid) so they fit perfectly, no matter how you resize it.

Here are some tips for using the grid:

- Prioritize content: Place the most important information in the first row or column, as this is what users will see first.
- Use different column widths: Combine columns of different widths to create a visually interesting layout.
- Nest rows and columns: Create more complex layouts by nesting rows and columns within each other.
- Use offsets: Create visual space and balance by offsetting columns.

2. Choose Responsive Charts

When selecting chart libraries or tools, make sure they offer responsive capabilities. This means the charts will automatically resize and adjust their layout to fit different screen sizes.

Think of it like a flexible image: It scales proportionally without losing quality.

Here are some responsive chart libraries:

- **Chart.js**: Offers responsive options and can be easily integrated with Bootstrap.
- **Highcharts**: A commercial library with excellent responsive features and a wide range of chart types.
- **Google Charts**: Provides responsive charts that can be customized with CSS.

3. Optimize for Mobile

Mobile devices have smaller screens and touch interfaces, so you need to pay special attention to the mobile experience.

Think of it like designing for a different planet: The rules are different, and you need to adapt your approach.

Here are some mobile optimization tips:

- Prioritize essential information: Display only the most critical data on smaller screens.

- Use larger touch targets: Make buttons and interactive elements larger and easier to tap.
- Simplify navigation: Use a clear and concise navigation menu that's easy to use on touchscreens.
- Consider touch gestures: Implement touch gestures like swiping or pinching to enhance interaction.

4. Test Thoroughly

Always test your dashboard on different devices and screen sizes to ensure it looks and functions correctly. Use browser developer tools to simulate different screen resolutions and identify any potential issues.

Think of it like a dress rehearsal: Make sure everything is perfect before the big show.

5. Leverage Bootstrap's Responsive Utilities

Bootstrap provides a variety of responsive utilities that can help you fine-tune your dashboard's layout. These utilities allow you to control the visibility, display, and spacing of elements at different breakpoints.

Think of it like a set of fine-tuning knobs: Use them to adjust the layout until it's just right.

Here are some useful responsive utilities:

- d-{breakpoint}-{value}: Control the display of elements at different breakpoints (e.g., d-none d-md-block hides an element on small screens but shows it on medium screens and larger).
- order-{breakpoint}-{value}: Change the order of elements at different breakpoints.
- m-{breakpoint}-{value} and p-{breakpoint}-{value}: Control margins and padding at different breakpoints.

Illustrating a Dynamic and Responsive Dashboard

Imagine a dashboard with a grid layout that adapts seamlessly to different screen sizes. On larger screens, the dashboard displays multiple charts and widgets side-by-side. As the screen size decreases, the layout adjusts, and the elements stack vertically. The charts resize proportionally, and the touch targets become larger for easier interaction on mobile devices.

This dashboard effectively combines Bootstrap's grid system, responsive charts, and mobile optimization techniques to create a dynamic and user-friendly experience on any device.

Experiment and Explore!

Creating dynamic and responsive dashboards is an iterative process. Experiment with different layouts, chart options, and responsive utilities to find the best solution for your specific needs. By following these guidelines and leveraging Bootstrap's powerful features, you can build dashboards that are both informative and engaging on any device.

In the next section, we'll put these principles into practice and build a responsive dashboard for our fictional "ZenHub" productivity app.

6.5 Project: Building an Analytics Dashboard with Interactive Charts

Alright, it's time to roll up our sleeves and build an interactive analytics dashboard using Bootstrap 5! We'll combine our knowledge of dashboard design, data visualization, and Bootstrap components to create a dynamic and informative tool.

For this project, we'll imagine we're building a dashboard for a fictional e-commerce store called "Trendy Threads." This dashboard will display key metrics like website traffic, sales performance, and customer demographics.

1. Planning the Dashboard

Before we dive into the code, let's plan out the structure and features of our dashboard:

Layout: We'll use a two-column layout with a sidebar on the left and the main content area on the right.

Charts: We'll include several interactive charts:

- Line chart: To show website traffic over time.

- Bar chart: To compare sales figures for different product categories.
- Pie chart: To display the distribution of customers by age group.

Filters: We'll add filters to allow users to:

- Select a date range for the data.
- Filter sales data by product category.

2. Setting Up the Structure

Create a new HTML file named dashboard.html and add the basic HTML structure, including the Bootstrap 5 CSS and JavaScript files.

HTML

```
<!DOCTYPE html>
<html lang="en">
<head>
    <meta charset="UTF-8">
    <meta name="viewport" content="width=device-width, initial-scale=1.0">
    <title>Trendy Threads - Analytics Dashboard</title>
    <link
href="https://cdn.jsdelivr.net/npm/bootstrap@5.3.0/dist/css/bootstra
```

```
p.min.css"            rel="stylesheet"            integrity="sha384-
9ndCyUaIbzAi2FUVXJi0CjmCapSmO7SnpJef0486qhLnuZ2cdeRhO02iuK6FUUVM"
crossorigin="anonymous">
    <link                                            rel="stylesheet"
href="https://cdn.jsdelivr.net/npm/bootstrap-
icons@1.10.3/font/bootstrap-icons.css"> </head>
<body>
    <script
src="https://cdn.jsdelivr.net/npm/bootstrap@5.3.0/dist/js/bootstrap.
bundle.min.js"                                      integrity="sha384-
geWF76RCwLtnZ8qwWowPQNguL3RmwHVBC9FhGdlKrxdiJJigb/j/68SIy3Te4Bkz"
crossorigin="anonymous"></script>
</body>
</html>
```

3. Building the Layout

Use Bootstrap's grid system to create the two-column layout:

HTML

```
<div class="container-fluid">
  <div class="row">
    <nav id="sidebarMenu" class="col-md-3 col-lg-2 d-md-block bg-
light sidebar collapse">
      <div class="position-sticky pt-3">
        <ul class="nav flex-column">
          <li class="nav-item">
            <a class="nav-link active" aria-current="page" href="#">
```

```
            <i class="bi bi-house"></i>
            Dashboard
          </a>
        </li>
        </ul>
      </div>
    </nav>

    <main class="col-md-9 ms-sm-auto col-lg-10 px-md-4">
      <div class="d-flex justify-content-between flex-wrap flex-md-nowrap align-items-center pt-3 pb-2 mb-3 border-bottom">
        <h1 class="h2">Dashboard</h1>
      </div>

      </main>
  </div>
</div>
```

This code creates a sidebar with a navigation menu and a main content area.

4. Adding the Charts

We'll use Chart.js to create the interactive charts. Include the Chart.js library in your HTML:

HTML
```
<script src="https://cdn.jsdelivr.net/npm/chart.js"></script>
```

Then, add the following code to the main section to create the charts:

HTML

```
<canvas id="trafficChart"></canvas>

<canvas id="salesChart"></canvas>
<canvas id="customerChart"></canvas>
```

This code creates three canvas elements where the charts will be rendered.

5. Implementing the Charts with JavaScript

Add the following JavaScript code to initialize the charts:

JavaScript

```
// Get the canvas elements

const trafficCanvas = document.getElementById('trafficChart');

const salesCanvas = document.getElementById('salesChart');

const customerCanvas = document.getElementById('customerChart');


// Create the charts

new Chart(trafficCanvas, {

  type: 'line',

  data: {

    // Your traffic data here...

  },

  options: {
```

```
    // Your chart options here...
  }
});

new Chart(salesCanvas, {
  type: 'bar',
  data: {
    // Your sales data here...
  },
  options: {
    // Your chart options here...
  }
});

new Chart(customerCanvas, {
  type: 'pie',
  data: {
    // Your customer data here...
  },
  options: {
    // Your chart options here...
  }
});
```

Replace the comments with your actual data and chart options.

6. Adding Filters

Add form controls to the sidebar to create the filters:

HTML

```html
<div class="position-sticky pt-3">
  <ul class="nav flex-column">
    <li class="nav-item">
      <a class="nav-link active" aria-current="page" href="#">
        <i class="bi bi-house"></i>
        Dashboard
      </a>
    </li>
    <li class="nav-item">
      <div class="form-floating mb-3">
        <input type="date" class="form-control" id="startDate"
placeholder="Start Date">
        <label for="startDate">Start Date</label>
      </div>
    </li>
    <li class="nav-item">
      <div class="form-floating mb-3">
        <input type="date" class="form-control" id="endDate"
placeholder="End Date">
        <label for="endDate">End Date</label>
      </div>
    </li>
```

```
    <li class="nav-item">
      <select class="form-select" id="categorySelect">
        <option selected>All Categories</option>
        <option value="1">Category 1</option>
        <option value="2">Category 2</option>
      </select>
    </li>
  </ul>
</div>
```

This code adds date range and category filters to the sidebar.

7. Making the Charts Interactive

Use JavaScript to update the charts based on the filter selections. You'll need to fetch the filtered data from your data source and update the chart data accordingly.

8. Running the Code

Save your dashboard.html file and open it in your web browser. You should see an interactive analytics dashboard with charts that update dynamically based on the filter selections.

Illustrating the Interface:

Imagine a dashboard with a sidebar on the left containing date range and category filters. The main content area displays three charts: a line chart showing website traffic over time, a bar chart comparing sales figures for different product categories, and a pie chart displaying the distribution of customers by age group.

Users can interact with the filters to update the charts and explore different aspects of the data. The charts are responsive and resize to fit the screen, providing a seamless experience on any device.

Congratulations! You've just built an interactive analytics dashboard with Bootstrap 5 and Chart.js. This project demonstrates how to combine dashboard design principles, data visualization techniques, and Bootstrap components to create a powerful and engaging data exploration tool.

Remember to experiment with different chart types, filters, and customization options to create dashboards that perfectly suit your specific needs and data.

CHAPTER 7: A DEEP DIVE INTO BOOTSTRAP 5 COMPONENTS

7.1 Understanding Component Structure and Functionality

Alright, it's time to roll up our sleeves and delve deeper into the heart of Bootstrap 5: its components! We've already used some of them in previous chapters, but now we'll take a closer look at how they're structured and how you can customize them to fit your needs.

Think of Bootstrap components as pre-fabricated building blocks for your website. They come in various shapes and sizes, ready to be assembled and customized to create unique and functional user interfaces.

Anatomy of a Component

Most Bootstrap components consist of a combination of HTML, CSS, and sometimes JavaScript. Let's break down the typical structure:

1. HTML: This provides the basic structure and content of the component. It defines the elements, attributes, and relationships between them.

- For example, a button component might consist of a <button> element with specific classes and attributes.

2. CSS: This styles the component, controlling its appearance, layout, and responsiveness.

- Bootstrap's CSS provides default styles for each component, ensuring consistency and visual appeal.

3. JavaScript: Some components require JavaScript to add interactive functionality.

- For example, a modal component uses JavaScript to show and hide the modal window, handle user interactions, and provide dynamic behavior.

Exploring Component Variations

Bootstrap offers a wide range of component variations to suit different needs and design preferences. These variations are often achieved through a combination of CSS classes and modifiers.

Here are some examples:

- **Buttons**: Bootstrap provides various button styles (primary, secondary, success, danger, etc.), sizes (small, large), and states (active, disabled).
- **Alerts**: Alerts come in different contextual variations (primary, secondary, success, danger, etc.) and can be dismissible.
- **Navbars**: Navbars can be styled with different color schemes, positioned at the top or bottom of the viewport, and include various elements like forms, buttons, or dropdown menus.

Understanding Component Functionality

Each Bootstrap component has its own specific functionality and behavior. It's important to understand how each component works and how it interacts with other components and the overall page layout.

For example:

- **Modals**: Modals are designed to display content in a pop-up window that overlays the main page content. They can be used for various purposes, such as displaying forms, alerts, or images.
- **Carousels**: Carousels are used to display a rotating set of images or content. They provide controls for navigating between slides and can be customized with different animations and transitions.
- **Dropdowns**: Dropdowns provide a way to display a list of options in a compact and user-friendly manner. They can be triggered by buttons, links, or other elements.

Inspecting Component Code

One of the best ways to understand Bootstrap components is to inspect their code. You can use your browser's developer tools to view the HTML, CSS, and JavaScript that make up a component.

This allows you to see how the component is structured, how the styles are applied, and how the JavaScript functions are used. You can also experiment with modifying the code to see how it affects the component's appearance and behavior.

Illustrating Component Structure

Let's take a closer look at the structure of a simple button component:

HTML
```html
<button type="button" class="btn btn-primary">Primary</button>
```

In this code:

<button> is the HTML element that creates the button.

type="button" specifies that the button is a standard button (not a submit or reset button).

class="btn btn-primary" applies the necessary CSS classes to style the button.

- btn is the base class for all Bootstrap buttons.
- btn-primary applies the primary button style (blue background).

By understanding the HTML, CSS, and JavaScript that make up Bootstrap components, you can gain a deeper understanding of how they work and how to customize them to fit your needs.

In the next section, we'll explore how to customize Bootstrap components using CSS and Sass.

7.2 Customizing Existing Components

Alright, now that we have a good grasp of Bootstrap 5's component structure, let's dive into the exciting world of customization! Think of it like this: you've got a toolbox full of high-quality tools (Bootstrap components), but you might need to adjust them slightly to fit your specific project or add your personal touch.

Bootstrap's components are designed to be flexible and customizable. You can modify their appearance, behavior, and even their underlying HTML structure to create unique and engaging user interfaces.

Here are some common approaches to customizing Bootstrap components:

1. CSS Overrides

The most straightforward way to customize components is by overriding their default CSS styles. You can use your own CSS rules to modify colors, fonts, sizes, spacing, and other visual aspects.

Think of it like adding a fresh coat of paint to a room: You're not changing the structure, but you're giving it a new look.

Here's an example of overriding the default button color:

```css
.btn-primary {
  background-color: #663399; /* Your custom color */
  border-color: #663399;
}
```

This CSS rule targets the .btn-primary class and changes the background and border colors to a custom purple shade.

Remember to place your custom CSS file after the Bootstrap CSS file in your HTML to ensure your styles take precedence.

2. Sass Variables and Mixins

For more extensive customization, you can leverage Sass variables and mixins. As we learned in Chapter 4, Sass allows you to modify Bootstrap's underlying variables and create reusable style blocks.

Think of it like having the blueprint for the house: You can modify the design and materials to create a custom build.

Here's an example of changing the default font family using a Sass variable:

SCSS
```
$font-family-sans-serif: 'Roboto', sans-serif;

@import "bootstrap/scss/bootstrap";
```

This code snippet modifies the $font-family-sans-serif variable, which controls the default font family used throughout Bootstrap.

3. Adding Custom Classes

You can add your own custom CSS classes to Bootstrap components to apply unique styles or modify their behavior. This allows you to create variations of existing components without altering **the core Bootstrap code.**

Think of it like adding accessories to an outfit: You're not changing the clothes themselves, but you're adding personal touches to create a unique look.

Here's an example of adding a custom class to a button:

HTML
```html
<button type="button" class="btn btn-primary btn-rounded">Rounded Button</button>
```

Then, in your CSS file, you can define the styles for the .btn-rounded class:

CSS
```css
.btn-rounded {
  border-radius: 20px; /* Add rounded corners */
}
```

4. Modifying HTML Structure

For more advanced customization, you can modify the HTML structure of a component. This allows you to add or remove elements, change their order, or nest components within each other.

Think of it like remodeling a room: You're changing the layout and structure to create a new space.

However, be cautious when modifying the HTML structure, as it can affect the component's functionality and compatibility with future Bootstrap updates.

5. JavaScript Customization

Some components, like modals or carousels, rely on JavaScript for their functionality. You can customize these components by modifying their JavaScript options or writing your own JavaScript code to interact with them.

Think of it like reprogramming the remote control: You're changing how the component responds to user input.

Illustrating Component Customization

Imagine you want to create a custom alert component with a unique color scheme and a larger font size. You can achieve this by:

1. **Overriding CSS**: Create CSS rules to change the background color, border color, and text color of the alert.

2. **Adding a custom class**: Add a custom class to the alert (e.g., .alert-lg) and define CSS rules to increase the font size.

This approach allows you to create a custom alert variation without modifying the core Bootstrap code.

Experiment and Explore!

Customizing Bootstrap components is a powerful way to create unique and engaging user interfaces. Experiment with different approaches, combine CSS overrides with Sass variables, add custom classes, and explore the possibilities of JavaScript customization.

In the next section, we'll delve even deeper into component customization by exploring how to create your own custom components from scratch.

7.3 Creating New Components with Sass and JavaScript

Alright, we've customized existing Bootstrap components, but now it's time to unleash our creativity and build our own custom components from scratch! This is where we truly become architects of our user interface, crafting unique elements that perfectly match our vision and functionality needs.

Think of it like this: instead of just modifying pre-fabricated furniture, we're designing and building our own custom pieces to perfectly fit our space and style.

Creating new components with Sass and JavaScript involves a blend of HTML structure, CSS styling, and JavaScript behavior. Let's break down the process:

1. Define the Purpose and Functionality

Before writing any code, clearly define:

- **What will the component do?** What problem will it solve or what task will it perform?

- **What will it look like?** Sketch out a visual representation of the component.
- **How will users interact with it?** Will it have any interactive elements or dynamic behavior?

For example, let's say we want to create a custom "notification card" component that displays important messages to the user. It should have a distinct visual style, an optional close button, and the ability to display different types of notifications (e.g., info, warning, error).

2. Structure the HTML

Create the HTML structure for your component. Use semantic HTML elements to define the component's structure and content.

For our notification card, the HTML might look like this:

```html
<div class="notification-card">
  <div class="notification-card-header">
    <span class="notification-card-title">Important
Message</span>
```

```
    <button type="button" class="btn-close" aria-label="Close"></button>
  </div>
  <div class="notification-card-body">
    <p>This is an important message for the user.</p>
  </div>
</div>
```

This code creates a basic structure with a header, title, close button, and body for the message.

3. Style with Sass

Use Sass to style your component. Define variables, mixins, and CSS rules to create the desired appearance and responsiveness.

For our notification card, we might define Sass variables for the background color, border color, and text color. We could also create mixins for different notification types (info, warning, error) that apply specific styles.

SCSS

```scss
$notification-bg: #f8f9fa;
$notification-border-color: #ced4da;
$notification-text-color: #343a40;
```

```
@mixin notification-info {
  background-color: lighten($notification-bg, 5%);
  border-color: lighten($notification-border-color, 5%);
}

// ... other mixins for warning and error
```

Then, apply these styles to the HTML structure using CSS rules:

SCSS

```
.notification-card {
  background-color: $notification-bg;
  border: 1px solid $notification-border-color;
  border-radius: 5px;
  padding: 15px;

  &-header {
    display: flex;
    justify-content: space-between;
    align-items: center;
    margin-bottom: 10px;
  }

  // ... other styles
}
```

4. Add JavaScript Behavior

If your component requires interactive functionality, use JavaScript to handle user interactions and dynamic behavior.

For our notification card, we might add JavaScript to:

- **Close the card:** When the close button is clicked, hide the card.
- **Change notification type:** Add a function to change the notification type (info, warning, error) and apply the corresponding styles.

JavaScript

```
const notificationCards =
document.querySelectorAll('.notification-card');

notificationCards.forEach(card => {
  const closeButton = card.querySelector('.btn-close');
  closeButton.addEventListener('click', () => {
    card.style.display = 'none';
  });

  // ... other JavaScript functions
});
```

5. Create a Reusable Component

To make your component reusable, encapsulate the HTML, CSS, and JavaScript into a single file or module. This allows you to easily include the component in different parts of your project or even share it with others.

You can create a separate HTML file for the component and include it using an <iframe> or use JavaScript frameworks like React or Vue.js to create reusable components.

Illustrating Component Creation

Imagine our custom notification card appearing at the top of a web page. It has a light gray background, a blue border, and a close button. When the user clicks the close button, the card smoothly fades out.

This component provides a visually appealing and user-friendly way to display notifications to the user.

In the next section, we'll explore how to organize and manage your custom components to create a reusable component library.

7.4 Building Reusable Component Libraries

Alright, we've mastered the art of creating custom Bootstrap 5 components. Now, let's take it a step further and organize those components into a reusable library! This is where we transform from component creators to component curators, building a collection of well-designed, readily available building blocks for our future projects.

Think of it like this: instead of scattering your tools all over the workshop, you're organizing them neatly into a toolbox, ready to be accessed and used whenever you need them.

Building a reusable component library offers several benefits:

- Efficiency: No need to reinvent the wheel every time you need a specific component.
- Consistency: Maintain a consistent look and feel across your projects.
- Maintainability: Update components in one place, and the changes will be reflected across all projects.

- Collaboration: Share your component library with other developers to foster collaboration and consistency.

Here's how to build your own reusable component library:

1. Choose a Structure

Decide how you want to organize your components. You can structure them by category (e.g., buttons, forms, navigation), functionality (e.g., modals, carousels, tooltips), or any other system that makes sense for your workflow.

Think of it like organizing your closet: You might organize clothes by type, season, or color.

Here are some common approaches:

- **Folders**: Create separate folders for different categories of components.
- **Naming conventions**: Use a consistent naming convention for your component files (e.g., button-primary.html, modal-lg.html).

- **Documentation**: Create a README file or a separate documentation website to explain how to use each component.

2. Encapsulate Components

Ensure each component is self-contained, including its HTML, CSS, and JavaScript in a single file or module. This makes it easier to include and reuse the component in different projects.

Think of it like a pre-packaged meal: It contains all the ingredients and instructions you need in one convenient package.

Here are some encapsulation techniques:

- HTML includes: Use server-side includes or client-side JavaScript to include component files in your projects.
- CSS modules: Use CSS modules or CSS-in-JS libraries to encapsulate component styles and prevent conflicts with other styles.
- JavaScript modules: Use JavaScript modules to encapsulate component logic and dependencies.

3. Create a Style Guide

Develop a style guide that defines the visual language and design principles for your components. This ensures consistency and helps maintain a cohesive look and feel across your projects.

Think of it like a brand book: It defines the colors, fonts, logos, and other visual elements that represent your brand.

Your style guide might include:

- **Color palette:** The primary and secondary colors used in your components.
- **Typography**: The font families, sizes, and weights used for headings, paragraphs, and other text elements.
- **Spacing**: The margins, padding, and grid system used to create layouts.
- **Component usage**: Guidelines on how to use each component and examples of best practices.

4. Version Control

Use a version control system like Git to track changes to your component library. This allows you to roll back to previous versions, collaborate with others, and manage updates effectively.

Think of it like a time machine for your code: You can go back to any point in the past and see how your components have evolved.

5. Testing and Documentation

Thoroughly test your components to ensure they work correctly in different contexts and browsers. Write clear and concise documentation to explain how to use each component, including its options, parameters, and dependencies.

Think of it like an instruction manual: It provides users with the information they need to use your components effectively.

Illustrating a Component Library

Imagine a folder named "components" in your project. Inside this folder, you have subfolders for "buttons," "forms," and "navigation." Each subfolder contains individual component files, such as button-primary.html, form-input.html, and navbar.html.

You also have a style-guide.md file that defines the design principles for your components and a README.md file that provides an overview of the library and instructions on how to use it.

This organized structure makes it easy to find, reuse, and maintain your components across different projects.

Experiment and Explore!

Building a reusable component library is an investment that will pay off in the long run. It streamlines your workflow, ensures consistency, and promotes collaboration.

Experiment with different organizational structures, encapsulation techniques, and documentation styles to create a component library that perfectly fits your needs and workflow.

By mastering this process, you'll transform from a Bootstrap user to a Bootstrap power user, creating a collection of custom components that will elevate your web development projects to new heights.

In the next section, we'll shift our focus to the world of JavaScript and explore how to add interactive functionality to your Bootstrap projects.

7.5 Project: Developing a Custom Modal Component with Advanced Features

Alright, let's put our component creation skills to the test and build a custom modal component with advanced features! We'll go beyond Bootstrap's basic modal and create one that's more flexible, customizable, and tailored to our specific needs.

Think of it like this: instead of settling for a standard pre-fabricated door, we're crafting a custom door with unique features like stained glass, intricate carvings, and a hidden lock.

Our custom modal will have the following features:

- Customizable size: Users can choose from different size options (small, medium, large).
- Optional header and footer: Users can include or exclude the header and footer sections.
- Close button variations: Users can choose different styles for the close button.
- Centered content: The modal content will be vertically centered.

- Smooth transitions: The modal will have smooth opening and closing animations.

1. HTML Structure

Let's start with the HTML structure for our custom modal:

HTML

```
<div class="custom-modal" tabindex="-1" aria-hidden="true">
  <div class="custom-modal-dialog">
    <div class="custom-modal-content">
      <div class="custom-modal-header">
        <h5 class="custom-modal-title">Modal Title</h5>
        <button type="button" class="btn-close" aria-
label="Close"></button>
      </div>
      <div class="custom-modal-body">
        <p>Modal body text goes here.</p>
      </div>
      <div class="custom-modal-footer">
        <button type="button" class="btn btn-
secondary">Close</button>
        <button type="button" class="btn btn-primary">Save
changes</button>
      </div>
    </div>
  </div>
</div>
```

This code creates a basic modal structure with a dialog, content area, header, body, and footer. We've used custom class names to distinguish our modal from Bootstrap's default modal.

2. CSS Styling

Now, let's add some CSS to style our modal:

```css
CSS
.custom-modal {
  display: none;
  position: fixed;
  z-index: 1050;
  top: 0;
  left: 0;
  width: 100%;
  height: 100%;
  overflow-x: hidden;
  overflow-y: auto;
  outline: 0;
}

.custom-modal-dialog {
  position: relative;
  width: auto;
  margin: 0.5rem;
  pointer-events: none;
```

```
}

.custom-modal-content {
  position: relative;
  display: flex;
  flex-direction: column;
  width: 100%;
  pointer-events: auto;
  background-color: #fff;
  background-clip: padding-box;
  border: 1px solid rgba(0, 0, 0, .2);
  border-radius: .3rem;
  outline: 0;
}

.custom-modal-header {
  display: flex;
  align-items: flex-start;
  justify-content: space-between;
  padding: 1rem;
  border-bottom: 1px solid #dee2e6;
  border-top-left-radius: calc(.3rem - 1px);
  border-top-right-radius: calc(.3rem - 1px);
}

.custom-modal-title {
  margin-bottom: 0;
```

```
  line-height: 1.5;
}

.custom-modal-body {
  position: relative;
  flex: 1 1 auto;
  padding: 1rem;
}

.custom-modal-footer {
  display: flex;
  flex-wrap: wrap;
  align-items: center;
  justify-content: flex-end;
  padding: .75rem;
  border-top: 1px solid #dee2e6;
  border-bottom-right-radius: calc(.3rem - 1px);
  border-bottom-left-radius: calc(.3rem - 1px);
}
```

This CSS code styles the modal with a white background, a border, and rounded corners. It also defines the layout for the header, body, and footer.

3. JavaScript Functionality

Now, let's add some JavaScript to handle the modal's behavior:

JavaScript

```
const customModal = document.querySelector('.custom-modal');
const modalDialog = customModal.querySelector('.custom-modal-dialog');
const modalContent = customModal.querySelector('.custom-modal-content');
const closeButton = customModal.querySelector('.btn-close');

// Function to show the modal
function showModal() {
  customModal.style.display = 'block';
  // Add class for animation
  setTimeout(() => {
    modalDialog.classList.add('show');
  }, 10);
}

// Function to hide the modal
function hideModal() {
  modalDialog.classList.remove('show');
  // Add a slight delay to allow animation to complete
  setTimeout(() => {
    customModal.style.display = 'none';
```

```
  }, 150);
}

// Event listener for the close button
closeButton.addEventListener('click', hideModal);

// Event listener to close the modal when clicking outside the
content area
customModal.addEventListener('click', (event) => {
  if (event.target === customModal &&
!modalContent.contains(event.target)) {
    hideModal();
  }
});
```

This JavaScript code defines functions to show and hide the modal and adds event listeners to the close button and the modal itself to handle closing.

4. Adding Advanced Features

Now, let's add the advanced features we outlined earlier:

- Customizable size: Add different CSS classes (e.g., .modal-sm, .modal-lg) to control the modal's size.
- Optional header and footer: Use JavaScript to conditionally show or hide the header and footer elements based on user preferences.
- Close button variations: Add different CSS classes (e.g., .btn-close-white, .btn-close-dark) to style the close button.
- Centered content: Use Flexbox to vertically center the modal content.
- Smooth transitions: Add CSS transitions to create smooth opening and closing animations.

5. Integrating with Bootstrap

You can integrate your custom modal with Bootstrap's existing JavaScript by triggering it with Bootstrap's data-bs-toggle="modal" and data-bs-target attributes. You'll need to modify the JavaScript to work with these attributes.

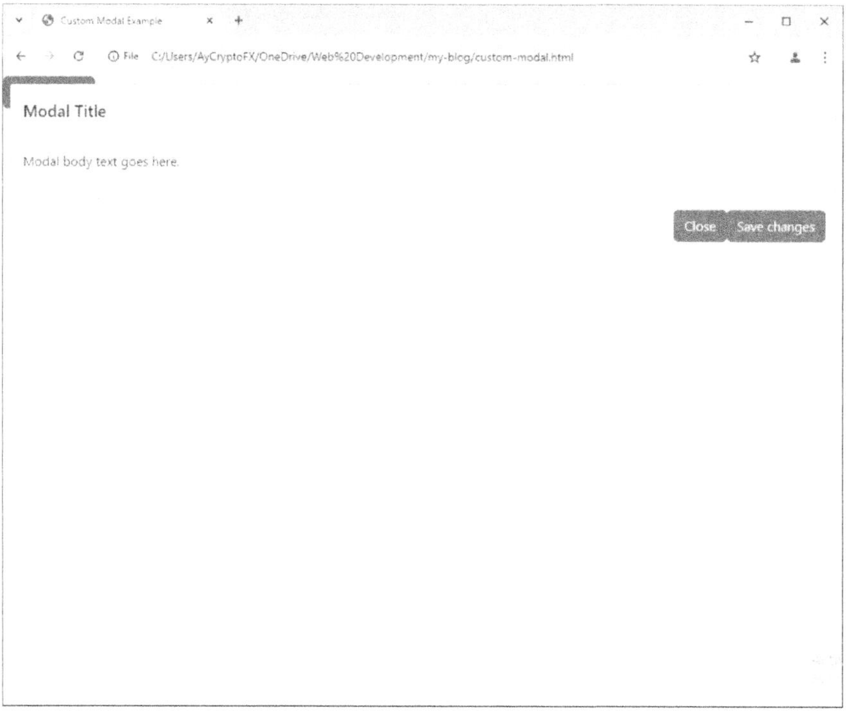

Source code

```
<!DOCTYPE html>
<html lang="en">
<head>
  <meta charset="UTF-8">
  <meta name="viewport" content="width=device-width, initial-
scale=1.0">
  <title>Custom Modal Example</title>
  <link
href="https://cdn.jsdelivr.net/npm/bootstrap@5.3.0/dist/css/
bootstrap.min.css"    rel="stylesheet"    integrity="sha384-
9ndCyUaIbzAi2FUVXJi0CjmCapSmO7SnpJef0486qhLnuZ2cdeRhO02iuK6F
UUVM" crossorigin="anonymous">
  <style>
    .custom-modal {
      display: none;
      position: fixed;
      z-index: 1050;
      top: 0;
      left: 0;
      width: 100%;
      height: 100%;
      overflow-x: hidden;
      overflow-y: auto;
      outline: 0;
      transition: opacity 0.15s linear;
```

```
}

.custom-modal-dialog {
  position: relative;
  width: auto;
  margin: 0.5rem;
  pointer-events: none;
  transition: transform 0.3s ease-out;
  transform: translateY(-50px);
}

.custom-modal.show .custom-modal-dialog {
  opacity: 1;
  transform: translateY(0);
}

.custom-modal-content {
  position: relative;
  display: flex;
  flex-direction: column;
  width: 100%;
  pointer-events: auto;
  background-color: #fff;
  background-clip: padding-box;
  border: 1px solid rgba(0, 0, 0, .2);
  border-radius: .3rem;
  outline: 0;
```

```
}

.custom-modal-header {
  display: flex;
  align-items: flex-start;
  justify-content: space-between;
  padding: 1rem;
  border-bottom: 1px solid #dee2e6;
  border-top-left-radius: calc(.3rem - 1px);
  border-top-right-radius: calc(.3rem - 1px);
}

.custom-modal-title {
  margin-bottom: 0;
  line-height: 1.5;
}

.custom-modal-body {
  position: relative;
  flex: 1 1 auto;
  padding: 1rem;
}

.custom-modal-footer {
  display: flex;
  flex-wrap: wrap;
  align-items: center;
```

```
      justify-content: flex-end;
      padding: .75rem;
      border-top: 1px solid #dee2e6;
      border-bottom-right-radius: calc(.3rem - 1px);
      border-bottom-left-radius: calc(.3rem - 1px);
    }

    .modal-lg .custom-modal-dialog {
      max-width: 800px;
    }

    .modal-sm .custom-modal-dialog {
      max-width: 300px;
    }

    .btn-close-white {
      filter: invert(1) grayscale(100%) brightness(200%);
    }
  </style>
</head>
<body>

  <button type="button" class="btn btn-primary" onclick="showModal()">Open Modal</button>

  <div class="custom-modal" tabindex="-1" aria-hidden="true">
    <div class="custom-modal-dialog modal-lg">
```

```
      <div class="custom-modal-content">
        <div class="custom-modal-header">
          <h5 class="custom-modal-title">Modal Title</h5>
          <button type="button" class="btn-close btn-close-
white" aria-label="Close"></button>
        </div>
        <div class="custom-modal-body">
          <p>Modal body text goes here.</p>
        </div>
        <div class="custom-modal-footer">
          <button type="button" class="btn btn-secondary"
onclick="hideModal()">Close</button>
          <button type="button" class="btn btn-primary">Save
changes</button>
        </div>
      </div>
    </div>
  </div>

  <script
src="https://cdn.jsdelivr.net/npm/bootstrap@5.3.0/dist/js/bo
otstrap.bundle.min.js"                    integrity="sha384-
geWF76RCwLtnZ8qwWowPQNguL3RmwHVBC9FhGdlKrxdiJJigb/j/68SIy3Te
4Bkz" crossorigin="anonymous"></script>
  <script>
    const customModal = document.querySelector('.custom-
modal');
```

```
    const modalDialog = customModal.querySelector('.custom-modal-dialog');
    const modalContent = customModal.querySelector('.custom-modal-content');
    const closeButton = customModal.querySelector('.btn-close');

    function showModal() {
      customModal.style.display = 'block';
      setTimeout(() => {
        customModal.classList.add('show');
        modalDialog.classList.add('show');
      }, 10);
    }

    function hideModal() {
      modalDialog.classList.remove('show');
      customModal.classList.remove('show');
      setTimeout(() => {
        customModal.style.display = 'none';
      }, 150);
    }

    closeButton.addEventListener('click', hideModal);

    customModal.addEventListener('click', (event) => {
```

```
      if (event.target === customModal &&
!modalContent.contains(event.target)) {
        hideModal();
      }
    });
  </script>
</body>
</html>
```

Illustrating the Custom Modal

Imagine a modal window appearing on the screen with a smooth fade-in animation. The modal has a custom purple background, a white close button, and a vertically centered content area. The user can close the modal by clicking the close button or clicking outside the modal.

This custom modal provides a more polished and tailored user experience compared to Bootstrap's default modal.

Part III: Advanced Techniques and Optimization

CHAPTER 8: JAVASCRIPT AND BOOTSTRAP 5

8.1 JavaScript Fundamentals (for Beginners)

Alright, let's dive into the world of JavaScript! This powerful scripting language is the engine that drives interactivity on the web. Think of it as the brain of your website – it brings your static HTML and CSS to life with dynamic behavior and user engagement.

While Bootstrap 5 provides a lot of functionality out of the box, JavaScript allows you to take it to the next level. You can create custom interactions, handle user input, and build truly dynamic web applications.

If you're new to JavaScript, don't worry! This section will provide a gentle introduction to the fundamentals, giving you the foundation you need to start adding interactivity to your Bootstrap projects.

What is JavaScript?

JavaScript is a scripting language that allows you to add interactivity and dynamic behavior to your web pages. It can do things like:

- **Change the content of a web page**: Update text, images, or other elements dynamically.
- **Respond to user actions**: React to clicks, mouseovers, or other user interactions.
- **Validate user input**: Check if data entered in a form is valid.
- **Make calculations**: Perform mathematical operations and manipulate data.
- **Communicate with servers**: Send and receive data from web servers without reloading the page.

Basic JavaScript Syntax

JavaScript code is written in plain text and is typically embedded within your HTML document using the <script> tag.

Here's a simple example:

HTML

```
<!DOCTYPE html>
<html>
<head>
  <title>My First JavaScript</title>
</head>
<body>

  <script>
    alert("Hello, world!");
  </script>

</body>
</html>
```

This code will display an alert box with the message "Hello, world!" when the page loads.

Let's break down some basic JavaScript syntax:

- **Statements**: JavaScript code consists of statements, which are instructions that tell the browser what to do. Statements are typically separated by semicolons (;).

- **Variables**: Variables are containers that store data. You can declare a variable using the var, let, or const keyword.
- **Data types**: JavaScript supports various data types, including numbers, strings, booleans, objects, and arrays.
- **Operators**: Operators are symbols that perform operations on data (e.g., + for addition, - for subtraction, = for assignment).
- **Functions**: Functions are reusable blocks of code that perform specific tasks. You can define a function using the function keyword.
- **Events**: Events are actions that occur on a web page, such as a mouse click or a key press. You can use event listeners to trigger JavaScript code when an event occurs.

JavaScript in Action

Let's see a more practical example of JavaScript in action:

HTML

```
<!DOCTYPE html>
<html>
<head>
  <title>JavaScript Example</title>
</head>
<body>

  <button onclick="changeText()">Click me</button>
  <p id="myParagraph">This is a paragraph.</p>

  <script>
    function changeText() {
      document.getElementById("myParagraph").innerHTML =
"The text has changed!";
    }
  </script>

</body>
</html>
```

This code creates a button that, when clicked, changes the text of a paragraph.

Here's how it works:

1. The onclick attribute of the button triggers the changeText() function when the button is clicked.
2. The changeText() function uses document.getElementById("myParagraph") to select the paragraph element with the ID "myParagraph."
3. The innerHTML property is used to change the content of the paragraph to "The text has changed!"

JavaScript and Bootstrap 5

JavaScript plays a crucial role in many Bootstrap 5 components, such as:

- **Modals**: JavaScript controls the showing and hiding of modals, as well as handling user interactions within the modal.
- **Carousels**: JavaScript manages the sliding animations and navigation controls of carousels.
- **Dropdowns**: JavaScript handles the toggling of dropdown menus and the selection of options.

- **Tooltips and Popovers**: JavaScript displays tooltips and popovers when users hover over or click on elements.

By understanding JavaScript fundamentals, you can customize these components, create your own interactive elements, and build dynamic web applications with Bootstrap 5.

In the next section, we'll delve deeper into how JavaScript interacts with Bootstrap 5 and explore how to use Bootstrap's JavaScript plugins to add interactive functionality to your projects.

8.2 Using Bootstrap 5's JavaScript Plugins

Alright, now that you've got a handle on JavaScript basics, let's explore how to supercharge your Bootstrap 5 projects with its built-in JavaScript plugins! These plugins provide interactive functionality for various components, like modals, dropdowns, tooltips, and more. Think of them as add-ons that enhance the user experience and bring your website to life.

The beauty of Bootstrap's JavaScript plugins is that they're designed to be easy to use. You can activate most of them with just a few lines of code or even with data attributes directly in your HTML. This means you can add dynamic behavior to your website without writing complex JavaScript from scratch.

1. Including the JavaScript Files

Before you can use the plugins, you need to include the necessary JavaScript files in your HTML document. You have two options:

- **Include the entire Bootstrap bundle**: This includes all of Bootstrap's JavaScript plugins in a single file.

HTML

```
<script
src="https://cdn.jsdelivr.net/npm/bootstrap@5.3.0/dist/js/bo
otstrap.bundle.min.js"                    integrity="sha384-
geWF76RCwLtnZ8qwWowPQNguL3RmwHVBC9FhGdlKrxdiJJigb/j/68SIy3Te
4Bkz" crossorigin="anonymous"></script>
```

- **Include individual plugin files**: If you only need specific plugins, you can include them individually. This can improve performance by reducing the amount of JavaScript loaded.

HTML

```
<script src="js/dist/modal.js"></script>
<script src="js/dist/dropdown.js"></script>
```

2. Activating Plugins with Data Attributes

The easiest way to activate Bootstrap plugins is by using data attributes directly in your HTML. This approach is called "data-driven activation."

For example, to activate a modal, you would add the following attributes to the modal's trigger element (usually a button):

HTML

```
<button type="button" class="btn btn-primary" data-bs-
toggle="modal" data-bs-target="#myModal">
  Launch demo modal
</button>
```

In this code:

- data-bs-toggle="modal" tells Bootstrap to activate the modal plugin.
- data-bs-target="#myModal" specifies the ID of the modal element to be shown.

Similarly, you can activate other plugins like tooltips, popovers, and carousels using data attributes. Refer to the Bootstrap documentation for the specific data attributes for each plugin.

3. Activating Plugins with JavaScript

You can also activate Bootstrap plugins programmatically using JavaScript. This gives you more control and flexibility, especially if you need to initialize plugins dynamically or based on certain conditions.

For example, to activate a tooltip, you would use the following JavaScript code:

JavaScript

```
const tooltipTriggerList = document.querySelectorAll('[data-bs-toggle="tooltip"]')
const tooltipList = [...tooltipTriggerList].map(tooltipTriggerEl => new bootstrap.Tooltip(tooltipTriggerEl))
```

This code selects all elements with the data-bs-toggle="tooltip" attribute and initializes a tooltip for each of them.

4. Exploring Popular Plugins

Let's take a closer look at some of the most popular Bootstrap JavaScript plugins:

- **Modal**: Displays content in a pop-up window that overlays the main page.
- **Dropdown**: Creates interactive dropdown menus.
- **Tooltip**: Displays small informational popups when users hover over elements.

- **Popover**: Similar to tooltips, but can contain more content and interactive elements.
- **Carousel**: Creates a slideshow of images or content.
- **Scrollspy**: Automatically updates navigation links based on the user's scroll position.
- **Toast**: Displays lightweight notifications that disappear after a certain time.

5. Illustrating Plugin Usage

Imagine a website with a button that triggers a modal window. When the user clicks the button, a modal appears with a form for submitting feedback. The modal also has a close button that allows the user to dismiss it.

This is a common example of how Bootstrap's modal plugin can be used to create interactive elements on a web page.

In the next section, we'll move beyond using pre-built plugins and explore how to create your own custom interactive components with JavaScript.

8.3 Creating Interactive Components with JavaScript

Alright, we've explored Bootstrap's JavaScript plugins, but now let's take our JavaScript skills to the next level and create our own interactive components! This is where we truly unleash the power of JavaScript to build dynamic and engaging user experiences.

Think of it like this: instead of just playing with pre-made toys, we're now designing and building our own, adding custom features and functionalities that bring our web pages to life.

Creating interactive components with JavaScript involves a blend of HTML structure, CSS styling, and JavaScript behavior. Let's break down the process:

1. Define the Purpose and Functionality

Before diving into code, clearly define:

- **What will the component do?** What user problem does it solve, or what task does it perform?

- **How should it look?** Sketch a visual representation of the component.
- **How will users interact with it?** What are the interactive elements and expected behaviors?

For example, let's say we want to create an interactive "accordion" component that expands and collapses sections of content. Users should be able to click on a heading to reveal or hide the content associated with it.

2. Structure the HTML

Create the HTML structure for your component using semantic elements.

For our accordion, the HTML might look like this:

HTML

```
<div class="accordion" id="myAccordion">
  <div class="accordion-item">
    <h2 class="accordion-header" id="headingOne">
      <button class="accordion-button" type="button" data-bs-toggle="collapse" data-bs-target="#collapseOne" aria-expanded="true" aria-controls="collapseOne">
        Accordion Item #1
      </button>
    </h2>
```

```
    <div id="collapseOne" class="accordion-collapse collapse
show"           aria-labelledby="headingOne"          data-bs-
parent="#myAccordion">
      <div class="accordion-body">
        This is the first item's accordion body.
      </div>
    </div>
  </div>
  <div class="accordion-item">
    <h2 class="accordion-header" id="headingTwo">
      <button       class="accordion-button       collapsed"
type="button"       data-bs-toggle="collapse"       data-bs-
target="#collapseTwo"      aria-expanded="false"       aria-
controls="collapseTwo">
        Accordion Item #2
      </button>
    </h2>
    <div id="collapseTwo" class="accordion-collapse collapse"
aria-labelledby="headingTwo" data-bs-parent="#myAccordion">
      <div class="accordion-body">
        This is the second item's accordion body.
      </div>
    </div>
  </div>
</div>
```

This code creates a basic accordion structure with two items, each with a header and collapsible content.

3. Style with CSS

Use CSS to style your component. For our accordion, we might add styles to customize the appearance of the headers, buttons, and content areas. We can leverage Bootstrap's existing utility classes or create our own custom styles.

CSS

```
.accordion-button {
  background-color: #f8f9fa; /* Light gray background */
  border: none;
}

.accordion-button:hover {
  background-color: #e2e6ea; /* Slightly darker on hover */
}

.accordion-button:focus {
  box-shadow: none; /* Remove default focus outline */
}

.accordion-body {
  background-color: #ffffff; /* White background for content
*/
}
```

4. Add JavaScript Behavior

Now, let's add the JavaScript that makes our accordion interactive:

JavaScript

```
const                    accordionHeaders                    =
document.querySelectorAll('.accordion-header button');

accordionHeaders.forEach(header => {
  header.addEventListener('click', () => {
    const accordionItem = header.closest('.accordion-item');
    const                    accordionBody                    =
accordionItem.querySelector('.accordion-body');

    // Toggle the 'show' class to expand/collapse the content
    accordionBody.classList.toggle('show');
```

```
    // Update the aria-expanded attribute for accessibility
    header.setAttribute('aria-expanded',
accordionBody.classList.contains('show'));
  });
});
```

This code selects all the accordion headers, attaches a click event listener to each, and toggles the visibility of the corresponding content area when clicked.

5. Enhance with Advanced Features

We can further enhance our accordion with features like:

- **Smooth transitions:** Use CSS transitions to create smooth expand/collapse animations.
- **Accessibility:** Ensure proper ARIA attributes are used for accessibility.
- **Dynamic content:** Load content dynamically using AJAX or fetch data from an API.
- **Custom events:** Trigger custom events when the accordion expands or collapses.

8.4 Integrating with JavaScript Frameworks (jQuery, React, Vue.js)

8.4.1 Component Wrapping and Data Binding

Alright, now that we've explored building interactive components with vanilla JavaScript, let's step into the world of JavaScript frameworks! These powerful tools provide structure, efficiency, and advanced capabilities for building complex web applications. Think of them as upgrading your toolbox with specialized power tools that make building intricate projects much easier.

In this section, we'll focus on integrating Bootstrap 5 with popular JavaScript frameworks like jQuery, React, and Vue.js. We'll explore how to wrap Bootstrap components within these frameworks and leverage their data binding capabilities to create dynamic and interactive user interfaces.

Why Use JavaScript Frameworks?

JavaScript frameworks offer several benefits over vanilla JavaScript:

- **Component-based architecture:** Frameworks like React, Vue.js, and Angular promote a component-based approach, allowing you to break down your UI into reusable and manageable components.
- **Data binding:** Frameworks provide mechanisms for efficiently synchronizing data between your application's logic and the user interface.
- **State management:** Frameworks offer tools for managing the state of your application, making it easier to handle complex interactions and data flows.
- **Virtual DOM:** Frameworks like React and Vue.js use a virtual DOM to optimize rendering performance, especially for complex applications.
- **Ecosystem and community:** Popular frameworks have thriving ecosystems with extensive libraries, tools, and community support.

Component Wrapping

Component wrapping involves taking a Bootstrap component and encapsulating it within a framework-specific component. This allows you to use the Bootstrap component within your framework's structure and leverage its data binding and other features.

Think of it like putting a beautiful handcrafted frame around a masterpiece painting: The frame enhances the presentation and integrates the painting into the overall decor.

Here's a basic example of wrapping a Bootstrap button within a React component:

JavaScript

```
import React from 'react';

function MyButton(props) {
  return (
    <button type="button" className={`btn btn-${props.color}`}>
      {props.children}
    </button>
  );
}

export default MyButton;
```

This code defines a React component called MyButton that wraps a Bootstrap button. The component accepts color and children props to customize the button's style and content.

You can then use this component in your React application like this:

JavaScript

```
import MyButton from './MyButton';

function MyComponent() {
  return (
    <div>
      <MyButton color="primary">Click me</MyButton>
    </div>
  );
}
```

Data Binding

Data binding is a powerful mechanism that allows you to synchronize data between your application's logic and the user interface. This means that changes to the data automatically update the UI, and user interactions with the UI can update the underlying data.

Think of it like a two-way mirror: You can see the reflection on both sides, and changes on one side are instantly reflected on the other.

Here's an example of data binding with a Bootstrap input field in Vue.js:

HTML

```
<template>
  <div>
    <input type="text" class="form-control" v-
model="name">
    <p>Your name is: {{ name }}</p>
  </div>
</template>

<script>
export default {
  data() {
    return {
      name: ''
    };
  }
};
</script>
```

This code creates an input field that is bound to the name data property. When the user types in the input field, the name property is automatically updated, and the change is reflected in the paragraph below.

Framework-Specific Considerations

Each JavaScript framework has its own nuances and best practices for integrating with Bootstrap.

- **jQuery:** jQuery is primarily a DOM manipulation library, so you can use it to interact with Bootstrap components and add custom behavior.
- **React:** React's component-based architecture makes it a natural fit for wrapping Bootstrap components and managing their state.
- **Vue.js:** Vue.js offers a flexible and approachable way to integrate Bootstrap components with its data binding and component system.

Experiment and Explore!

Integrating Bootstrap 5 with JavaScript frameworks opens up a world of possibilities for building complex and dynamic web applications. Experiment with different frameworks, explore their component wrapping and data binding capabilities, and discover how they can enhance your Bootstrap projects.

By mastering these techniques, you can create truly interactive and engaging user interfaces that leverage the power of both Bootstrap and your chosen JavaScript framework.

8.4.2 State Management and Reactivity

Alright, let's dive deeper into the world of JavaScript frameworks and explore the concepts of **state management** and **reactivity**. These are essential aspects of building complex and dynamic web applications, especially when integrating Bootstrap 5 with frameworks like React, Vue.js, or Angular.

Think of **state** as the memory of your application. It holds all the dynamic data that influences how your UI looks and behaves. This could include user input, data fetched from a server, or the current status of interactive elements.

State management is the process of organizing, updating, and accessing this state in a consistent and efficient way. It ensures that your UI stays in sync with the underlying data and that changes to the state are reflected accurately in the user interface.

Reactivity is the ability of the framework to automatically update the UI whenever the state changes. This means you don't have to manually manipulate the DOM (Document Object Model) to reflect changes in the data. The framework takes care of that for you, making your code cleaner and more efficient.

Why State Management Matters

As your application grows in complexity, managing state effectively becomes crucial. Without proper state management, you might encounter issues like:

- **Data inconsistencies:** Different parts of your UI might display outdated or conflicting data.
- **Difficult debugging:** Tracking down the source of data errors can be challenging.
- **Performance issues:** Inefficient state updates can lead to slow performance and a poor user experience.

State Management in Different Frameworks

Each JavaScript framework has its own approach to state management:

- **React:** React offers Context API and libraries like Redux or Zustand for managing state.
- **Vue.js:** Vue.js provides reactivity built-in with its data() property and offers Vuex for more complex state management.
- **Angular:** Angular uses RxJS and services to manage state and data flow.

Reactivity in Action

Let's illustrate reactivity with a simple example in React:

JavaScript

```
import React, { useState } from 'react';

function Counter() {
  const [count, setCount] = useState(0);

  return (
    <div>
      <p>You clicked {count} times</p>
      <button onClick={() => setCount(count + 1)}>
```

```
        Click me
      </button>
    </div>
  );
}
```

In this code:

- useState(0) initializes a state variable called count with a value of 0.
- The setCount function updates the value of count.
- Whenever setCount is called, React automatically re-renders the component, updating the UI to reflect the new value of count.

This demonstrates how reactivity ensures that the UI stays in sync with the state without manual DOM manipulation.

Benefits of Reactivity

Reactivity offers several advantages:

- **Simplified development:** You don't have to write code to manually update the DOM.

- **Improved performance:** Frameworks optimize state updates to minimize unnecessary re-renders.
- **Enhanced maintainability:** Your code becomes cleaner and easier to understand.
- **Reduced bugs:** Automatic UI updates reduce the risk of data inconsistencies.

Integrating with Bootstrap 5

When integrating Bootstrap 5 with JavaScript frameworks, you can leverage state management and reactivity to create dynamic and interactive components.

For example, you could:

- **Build a dynamic form:** Use state to store form data and update the UI based on user input.
- **Create an interactive dashboard:** Use state to manage data fetched from an API and display it in charts and graphs.
- **Develop a real-time chat application:** Use state to update the chat messages as they are received.

Experiment and Explore!

State management and reactivity are essential concepts in modern web development. Experiment with different state management solutions in your chosen framework and explore how reactivity simplifies development and enhances user experience.

By mastering these concepts, you can build complex and dynamic web applications with Bootstrap 5 and your favorite JavaScript framework.

8.4.3 Building Single-Page Applications with Bootstrap 5

Alright, let's explore the exciting world of **Single-Page Applications (SPAs)** and how you can build them using Bootstrap 5 and a JavaScript framework!

Think of a traditional website like a book. Each page is a separate chapter, and you navigate between them by turning pages. This involves loading a new HTML document for each page, which can sometimes be slow and disruptive.

Now, imagine a website that's like a single, long scroll. All the content is loaded at once, and you navigate between different sections seamlessly without reloading the page. This is the essence of a Single-Page Application (SPA).

SPAs offer several advantages:

- **Faster and smoother user experience:** No more waiting for pages to load – navigation is instant and seamless.
- **Improved performance:** Reduced server requests and optimized rendering can lead to faster loading times and better performance.
- **Dynamic and interactive:** SPAs can provide a more dynamic and interactive user experience, similar to a desktop application.
- **Offline capabilities:** SPAs can be designed to work offline, allowing users to access content even without an internet connection.

Building SPAs with Bootstrap 5

While Bootstrap 5 primarily focuses on styling and layout, it can be effectively combined with JavaScript frameworks to build SPAs. The framework handles the routing, data management, and dynamic updates, while Bootstrap provides the styling and components for the user interface.

Here's a breakdown of the key elements involved:

1. **JavaScript Framework:** Choose a JavaScript framework that supports SPA development, such as:
    - **React:** Popular for its component-based architecture and virtual DOM.
    - **Vue.js:** Known for its ease of use and flexibility.
    - **Angular:** A comprehensive framework with a strong emphasis on structure and scalability.
2. **Routing:** Implement routing to manage navigation between different views or sections of your SPA. This involves defining routes that map URLs to specific components or views.

   - Most frameworks offer built-in routing solutions or popular libraries like React Router (for React).

3. **Data Management:** Use the framework's state management capabilities or external libraries to manage the data in your SPA. This includes fetching data from APIs, updating the state based on user interactions, and ensuring data consistency across different views.

4. **Bootstrap Components:** Leverage Bootstrap 5's components to build the user interface of your SPA. Wrap Bootstrap components within your framework's component structure and use data binding to connect them to your application's state.

5. **API Integration:** If your SPA needs to interact with a server, use JavaScript's fetch API or libraries like Axios to make API calls and handle data exchange.

Example: Building a Simple SPA with React and Bootstrap 5

Let's imagine a simple SPA with two views: a "Home" view and an "About" view.

JavaScript

```
// App.js
import React from 'react';
import { BrowserRouter as Router, Routes, Route, Link } from
'react-router-dom';
import Home from './Home';
import About from './About';

function App() {
  return (
    <Router>
      <div>
        <nav className="navbar navbar-expand-lg navbar-light
bg-light">
          <ul className="navbar-nav">
            <li className="nav-item">
              <Link className="nav-link" to="/">Home</Link>
            </li>
            <li className="nav-item">
              <Link                      className="nav-link"
to="/about">About</Link>
            </li>
          </ul>
        </nav>

        <Routes>
          <Route path="/" element={<Home />} />
          <Route path="/about" element={<About />} />
        </Routes>
      </div>
    </Router>
  );
}

export default App;
```

JavaScript

```
// Home.js
import React from 'react';

function Home() {
  return (
    <div className="container">
      <h1>Welcome to the Home Page!</h1>
    </div>
  );
}

export default Home;
```

JavaScript

```
// About.js
import React from 'react';

function About() {
  return (
    <div className="container">
      <h1>About Us</h1>
      <p>This is a simple about page.</p>
    </div>
  );
}

export default About;
```

This code defines a simple SPA with two routes (/ for Home and /about for About). The App component renders the navigation bar and uses react-router-dom to handle routing. When the user clicks on the navigation links, the corresponding component is rendered without reloading the page.

8.4.4 Project: Building a To-Do List Application with React and Bootstrap 5

Alright, let's put our React and Bootstrap skills to the test and build a practical to-do list application! This project will combine our knowledge of component wrapping, data binding, state management, and Bootstrap's styling capabilities to create a dynamic and user-friendly task management tool.

Think of this as building your own personalized task command center, where you can add, delete, and manage your tasks with ease and style.

1. Setting up the Project

First, make sure you have Node.js and npm (or yarn) installed on your system. Then, create a new React project using Create React App:

Bash
```
npx create-react-app my-todo-app
cd my-todo-app
```

Next, install Bootstrap 5:

Bash
```
npm install bootstrap
```

Import Bootstrap's CSS into your src/index.js file:

JavaScript

```
import React from 'react';
import ReactDOM from 'react-dom/client';
import App from './App';
import 'bootstrap/dist/css/bootstrap.min.css';

const                          root                          =
ReactDOM.createRoot(document.getElementById('root'));
root.render(
  <React.StrictMode>
    <App />
  </React.StrictMode>
);
```

2. Building the Components

Let's create the following components:

- **App:** The main component that will hold the to-do list state and render other components.
- **TodoList:** A component to display the list of to-dos.
- **TodoItem:** A component to represent a single to-do item.

- **AddTodo:** A component to add new to-dos.

Here's the code for each component:

App.js:

JavaScript

```
import React, { useState, useEffect } from 'react';
import TodoList from './TodoList';
import AddTodo from './AddTodo';

function App() {
  const [todos, setTodos] = useState([]);

  useEffect(() => {
    // Load todos from local storage on component mount
    const storedTodos = localStorage.getItem('todos');
    if (storedTodos) {
      setTodos(JSON.parse(storedTodos));
    }
  }, []);

  useEffect(() => {
    // Save todos to local storage whenever todos array changes
    localStorage.setItem('todos', JSON.stringify(todos));
  }, [todos]);

  const addTodo = (newTodo) => {
    setTodos([...todos, { id: Date.now(), text: newTodo, completed:
false }]);
  };

  const deleteTodo = (id) => {
    setTodos(todos.filter(todo => todo.id !== id));
  };

  const toggleComplete = (id) => {
    setTodos(todos.map(todo =>
      todo.id === id ? { ...todo, completed: !todo.completed } : todo
    ));
  };
```

```
  return (
    <div className="container">
      <h1>My To-Do List</h1>
      <AddTodo addTodo={addTodo} />
      <TodoList          todos={todos}          deleteTodo={deleteTodo}
toggleComplete={toggleComplete} />
    </div>
  );
}

export default App;
```

TodoList.js:

JavaScript

```
import React from 'react';
import TodoItem from './TodoItem';

function TodoList({ todos, deleteTodo, toggleComplete }) {
  return (
    <ul className="list-group">
      {todos.map(todo => (
        <TodoItem
          key={todo.id}
          todo={todo}
          deleteTodo={deleteTodo}
          toggleComplete={toggleComplete}
        />
      ))}
    </ul>
  );
}

export default TodoList;
```

TodoItem.js:

JavaScript

```
import React from 'react';

function TodoItem({ todo, deleteTodo, toggleComplete }) {
  return (
    <li className={`list-group-item d-flex justify-content-between
align-items-center ${todo.completed ? 'text-decoration-line-through'
: ''}`}>
      <span                    onClick={()                    =>
toggleComplete(todo.id)}>{todo.text}</span>
      <button  className="btn  btn-danger  btn-sm"  onClick={()  =>
deleteTodo(todo.id)}>Delete</button>
    </li>
  );
}

export default TodoItem;
```

AddTodo.js:

JavaScript

```
import React, { useState } from 'react';

function AddTodo({ addTodo }) {
  const [newTodo, setNewTodo] = useState('');

  const handleSubmit = (e) => {
    e.preventDefault();
    if (newTodo.trim() !== '') {
      addTodo(newTodo);
      setNewTodo('');
    }
  };

  return (
```

```
    <form onSubmit={handleSubmit} className="mb-3">
      <div className="input-group">
        <input
          type="text"
          className="form-control"
          placeholder="Add a new to-do..."
          value={newTodo}
          onChange={(e) => setNewTodo(e.target.value)}
        />
        <button              className="btn              btn-primary"
type="submit">Add</button>
      </div>
    </form>
  );
}

export default AddTodo;
```

3. Running the Application

Start the development server:

Bash
```
npm start
```

This will open the to-do list application in your browser. You can now add new to-dos, mark them as complete, and delete them. The app will also save your to-dos to local storage so they persist even after you refresh the page.

Key takeaways:

- **Component wrapping:** We wrapped Bootstrap's form controls and list group components within React components.
- **Data binding:** We used React's state to manage the to-do list data and update the UI dynamically.
- **State management:** We used useState to manage the to-do list data and useEffect to persist data in local storage.
- **Bootstrap styling:** We used Bootstrap classes to style the to-do list and its components.

This project provides a solid foundation for building more complex applications with React and Bootstrap 5.

CHAPTER 9: THE UTILITY API

9.1 Understanding the Utility-First Approach

Alright, let's dive into a different way of thinking about CSS and styling: the **utility-first approach**. This methodology, popularized by frameworks like Tailwind CSS, challenges the traditional way we write CSS and offers a fresh perspective on building user interfaces.

Think of traditional CSS like building with Lego bricks. You have a box of various bricks, and you combine them to create different structures. You might have specific bricks for walls, windows, and roofs.

Now, imagine a box of Lego bricks where every brick is a single, atomic unit of styling, like a specific color, margin, or padding. This is the essence of the utility-first approach.

Instead of creating reusable CSS classes with multiple properties, you apply individual utility classes directly in your

HTML to style each element. These utility classes represent single CSS properties, like p-4 for padding, text-blue-500 for text color, or rounded-lg for rounded corners.

Benefits of Utility-First

This approach offers several advantages:

- **Rapid development:** Quickly style elements without writing custom CSS.
- **Consistency:** Enforce a consistent design system with a predefined set of utilities.
- **Maintainability:** Reduce CSS bloat and make it easier to update styles.
- **Responsiveness:** Easily create responsive designs with breakpoint-specific utilities.
- **Customization:** Configure the utility set to match your specific needs.

How it Works

1. **Predefined Utilities:** A utility-first framework provides a comprehensive set of pre-defined utility classes for common styling needs.

2. **HTML Application:** You apply these utility classes directly in your HTML, creating a chain of classes that define the element's style.

HTML

```
<button class="bg-blue-500 hover:bg-blue-700 text-white font-bold
py-2 px-4 rounded">
        Button
</button>
```

3. **No Custom CSS (Ideally):** The goal is to minimize or eliminate the need for writing custom CSS. The predefined utilities should cover most of your styling needs.

Bootstrap's Utility API

While Bootstrap 5 isn't strictly a utility-first framework, it embraces this approach with its **Utility API**. This API provides a set of Sass functions and mixins that allow you to generate utility classes dynamically.

This means you can:

- **Extend the default utilities:** Add new utilities for properties not covered by the default set.
- **Customize existing utilities:** Modify the values or behavior of existing utilities.
- **Create responsive variations:** Generate utilities that apply only at specific breakpoints.

Example: Creating a Custom Utility

Let's say you want to create a utility class for setting the font-style property to italic. You can use Bootstrap's map-merge and theme-color-level functions to achieve this:

SCSS

```
$utilities: map-merge(
  $utilities,
  (
    "font-style": (
      property: font-style,
      class: fst,
      values: (
        italic: italic,
      )
```

```
    )
  )
);
```

This code adds a new utility called fst-italic that sets the font-style to italic.

Illustrating the Utility-First Approach

Imagine styling a button with traditional CSS:

HTML

```html
<button class="my-button">Button</button>
```

CSS

```css
.my-button {
  background-color: blue;
  color: white;
  padding: 10px 20px;
  border-radius: 5px;
}
```

Now, imagine styling the same button with a utility-first approach:

HTML

```html
<button class="bg-blue-500 text-white px-4 py-2
rounded">Button</button>
```

Notice how the utility-first approach eliminates the need for a custom CSS class and directly applies the styles in the HTML.

Experiment and Explore!

The utility-first approach offers a different perspective on CSS and styling. While it might seem unconventional at first, it can significantly speed up development and improve maintainability.

Experiment with Bootstrap's Utility API, explore the possibilities of generating custom utilities, and discover how this approach can enhance your workflow.

9.2 Mastering Bootstrap 5's Utility Classes

Alright, let's dive deep into the practical side of Bootstrap 5's Utility API and master its vast collection of utility classes! These are the individual Lego bricks of styling that empower you to construct intricate layouts and designs without writing custom CSS.

Think of it like having a massive toolbox with every tool imaginable. Instead of crafting your own tools from scratch, you can simply reach into this toolbox and grab the perfect utility for the job.

Bootstrap 5 provides hundreds of utility classes that cover a wide range of CSS properties, including:

- **Spacing:** Margins, padding, and gaps between elements.
- **Sizing:** Widths, heights, and aspect ratios.
- **Typography:** Font sizes, weights, styles, and text alignment.
- **Colors:** Text colors, background colors, and border colors.

- **Borders:** Border widths, styles, and colors.
- **Display:** Display properties like block, inline, flex, and none.
- **Positioning:** Position properties like static, relative, absolute, and fixed.
- **Flexbox:** Flexbox properties for controlling layout and alignment within flex containers.
- **And much more!**

Understanding the Naming Convention

Bootstrap's utility classes follow a consistent naming convention that makes them easy to understand and remember. The general pattern is:

```
{property}-{breakpoint?}-{value}
```

- **property:** The CSS property being modified (e.g., m for margin, p for padding, bg for background-color).
- **breakpoint?** (optional): A breakpoint prefix to apply the utility only at specific screen sizes (e.g., sm, md, lg).

- **value:** The value of the CSS property (e.g., 1 for 1rem spacing, blue-500 for a specific shade of blue).

For example:

- mt-4: Applies a top margin of 4 units (4rem by default).
- p-lg-3: Applies padding of 3 units on large screens and wider.
- text-red-500: Sets the text color to a specific shade of red.

Exploring Common Utilities

Let's explore some of the most commonly used utility classes:

- **Spacing:**
  - m-{size}: Margin (e.g., mt-2 for top margin, mb-4 for bottom margin).
  - p-{size}: Padding (e.g., px-3 for horizontal padding, py-2 for vertical padding).
  - gap-{size}: Gap between elements in flex containers.

- **Sizing:**
  - w-{size}: Width (e.g., w-25 for 25% width, w-100 for full width).
  - h-{size}: Height (e.g., h-auto, h-100).
- **Typography:**
  - text-{size}: Font size (e.g., text-sm, text-lg).
  - font-{weight}: Font weight (e.g., font-bold, font-light).
  - text-{alignment}: Text alignment (e.g., text-center, text-end).
- **Colors:**
  - text-{color}: Text color (e.g., text-primary, text-danger).
  - bg-{color}: Background color (e.g., bg-light, bg-dark).
- **Borders:**
  - border: Adds a border.

- border-{side}: Adds a border to a specific side (e.g., border-top, border-end).
- border-{color}: Sets the border color (e.g., border-primary).
- rounded: Adds rounded corners.
- rounded-{size}: Adds rounded corners with different sizes (e.g., rounded-sm, rounded-lg).

Building Layouts with Utilities

You can combine utility classes to create complex layouts without writing any custom CSS. For example, to create a two-column layout with spacing and responsive behavior, you could use the following code:

HTML

```
<div class="container">
  <div class="row">
    <div class="col-md-6 bg-light p-4">
      Column 1
    </div>
    <div class="col-md-6 bg-white p-4 ms-md-2">
      Column 2
    </div>
  </div>
</div>
```

This code creates two columns that are equal width on medium-sized screens and larger. The columns have a light gray and white background, respectively, and are spaced apart with a margin.

Illustrating Utility Classes

Imagine styling a card component with utilities:

HTML

```
<div class="card bg-light shadow-sm p-3 mb-5 rounded">
  <div class="card-body">
    <h5 class="card-title text-primary">Card Title</h5>
    <p class="card-text">Some quick example text to build on the card
title and make up the bulk of the card's content.</p>
    <a href="#" class="btn btn-primary">Go somewhere</a>
  </div>
</div>
```

This code uses utility classes to style the card with a light gray background, a subtle shadow, padding, a rounded border, and a primary-colored title.

9.3 Building Custom Utilities with Sass

Alright, let's take our utility-first skills to the next level and build our own custom utilities with Sass! This is where we truly unlock the flexibility and power of Bootstrap 5's Utility API, tailoring it to our specific needs and design system.

Think of it like this: instead of just using the tools in the toolbox, we're now crafting our own specialized tools to perfectly fit the unique challenges of our projects.

Bootstrap's Utility API provides a set of Sass functions and mixins that make it surprisingly easy to generate custom utility classes. This allows us to:

- **Extend the default utilities:** Add new utilities for CSS properties not covered by Bootstrap's default set.
- **Customize existing utilities:** Modify the values or behavior of existing utilities to match our preferences.
- **Create responsive variations:** Generate utilities that apply only at specific breakpoints.

The add-utilities Mixin

The add-utilities mixin is the heart of Bootstrap's Utility API. It allows you to define new utilities or override existing ones. Here's the basic syntax:

SCSS

```
@use "sass:map";

$utilities: (
  "my-utility": (
    property: my-property,
    class: my-class,
    values: (
      value1: css-value1,
      value2: css-value2,
      // ...
    )
  )
);

@include add-utilities($utilities);
```

In this code:

- $utilities: A Sass map that defines the utilities you want to add or override.
- "my-utility": The name of the utility.

- property: The CSS property being modified (e.g., font-size, margin, color).
- class: The class name prefix for the utility (e.g., fs for font-size, m for margin).
- values: A map of values for the utility (e.g., sm: 1rem, lg: 2rem).

Example: Creating a Custom Spacing Utility

Let's say we want to create a custom spacing utility called my-space that adds margin to the top and bottom of an element. We can use the add-utilities mixin like this:

SCSS
```
@use "sass:map";

$utilities: (
  "my-space": (
    property: margin-top,
    class: my-space,
    values: (
      0: 0,
      1: 1rem,
      2: 2rem,
      3: 3rem,
    )
  )
);
```

```
@include add-utilities($utilities);
```

This code will generate the following utility classes:

- my-space-0: Sets margin-top: 0.
- my-space-1: Sets margin-top: 1rem.
- my-space-2: Sets margin-top: 2rem.
- my-space-3: Sets margin-top: 3rem.

We can then use these classes in our HTML like this:

HTML
```
<div class="my-space-2">This div has a top margin of 2rem.</div>
```

Responsive Variations

To create responsive variations of our custom utility, we can use the responsive option in the add-utilities mixin:

SCSS

```
@use "sass:map";

$utilities: (
  "my-space": (
    property: margin-top,
    class: my-space,
    responsive: true,
    values: (
      0: 0,
      1: 1rem,
```

```
      2: 2rem,
      3: 3rem,
    )
  )
);

@include add-utilities($utilities);
```

This will generate responsive variations for each breakpoint (e.g., my-space-sm-2, my-space-md-3).

Customizing Existing Utilities

We can also use the add-utilities mixin to customize existing Bootstrap utilities. For example, to change the default spacing values, we can override the spacing map:

SCSS

```
$spacers: (
  0: 0,
  1: 0.5rem, // Changed from 1rem
  2: 1rem,   // Changed from 2rem
  3: 1.5rem, // Changed from 3rem
  // ...
);
```

This will update the default spacing values used by utilities like mt, mb, p, etc.

Illustrating Custom Utilities

Imagine you're building a website with a unique design system that requires specific font sizes not covered by Bootstrap's default utilities. You can use the add-utilities mixin to create custom font size utilities that perfectly match your design requirements.

Experiment and Explore!

Building custom utilities with Sass gives you fine-grained control over your styling and allows you to create a truly bespoke design system. Explore the possibilities of the Utility API, experiment with different CSS properties, and create a library of custom utilities that perfectly match your needs and preferences.

By mastering this technique, you can extend Bootstrap's capabilities and create a truly personalized and efficient workflow for styling your web projects.

9.4 Project: Styling a Landing Page with Utility Classes

Alright, let's put our utility-first skills to the test and style a complete landing page using Bootstrap 5's utility classes! This project will demonstrate how to leverage the power of the Utility API to create a responsive and visually appealing design without writing custom CSS.

Think of it like assembling a stunning mosaic with pre-cut tiles. Each utility class is a tile, and we'll carefully arrange them to create a beautiful and harmonious composition.

Our landing page will promote our fictional "ZenHub" productivity app, featuring a hero section, feature highlights, testimonials, and a call to action.

1. Setting Up the Structure

Create a new HTML file named landing.html and add the basic HTML structure, including the Bootstrap 5 CSS file.

HTML

```
<!DOCTYPE html>
<html lang="en">
<head>
  <meta charset="UTF-8">
  <meta    name="viewport"    content="width=device-width,    initial-
scale=1.0">
  <title>ZenHub - Find Your Focus</title>
  <link
href="https://cdn.jsdelivr.net/npm/bootstrap@5.3.0/dist/css/bootstra
p.min.css"             rel="stylesheet"             integrity="sha384-
9ndCyUaIbzAi2FUVXJi0CjmCapSmO7SnpJef0486qhLnuZ2cdeRhO02iuK6FUUVM"
crossorigin="anonymous">
</head>
<body>

  <script
src="https://cdn.jsdelivr.net/npm/bootstrap@5.3.0/dist/js/bootstrap.
bundle.min.js"                                        integrity="sha384-
geWF76RCwLtnZ8qwWowPQNguL3RmwHVBC9FhGdlKrxdiJJigb/j/68SIy3Te4Bkz"
crossorigin="anonymous"></script>
</body>
</html>
```

2. Building the Hero Section

Let's start with a captivating hero section:

HTML

```
<section class="bg-blue-500 text-white py-10">
  <div class="container mx-auto text-center">
    <h1   class="text-5xl   font-bold   mb-4">Find   Your   Focus   with
ZenHub</h1>
    <p class="text-xl mb-8">Boost your productivity and achieve your
goals with our powerful task management app.</p>
    <button class="bg-white text-blue-500 hover:bg-blue-100 font-bold
py-3 px-6 rounded-lg">
      Download Now
    </button>
  </div>
</section>
```

This code creates a hero section with a blue background, white text, a large heading, a descriptive paragraph, and a prominent call-to-action button.

3. Showcasing Features

Next, let's highlight ZenHub's key features:

HTML

```
<section class="py-10">
  <div class="container mx-auto">
    <div class="grid grid-cols-1 md:grid-cols-3 gap-8">
      <div class="bg-white p-6 rounded-lg shadow-md">
        <h3 class="text-xl font-bold mb-4">Task Management</h3>
        <p>Organize your tasks, set deadlines, and track your progress
with ease.</p>
      </div>
      <div class="bg-white p-6 rounded-lg shadow-md">
        <h3 class="text-xl font-bold mb-4">Time Management</h3>
        <p>Maximize your productivity with time tracking, focus
modes, and break reminders.</p>
      </div>
      <div class="bg-white p-6 rounded-lg shadow-md">
        <h3 class="text-xl font-bold mb-4">Collaboration</h3>
        <p>Collaborate with your team on projects, share tasks, and
achieve common goals.</p>
      </div>
    </div>
  </div>
</section>
```

This code creates a three-column grid to showcase three key features. Each column features a heading and a brief description.

4. Adding Testimonials

Let's add some social proof with testimonials:

HTML

```
<section class="bg-gray-100 py-10">
  <div class="container mx-auto">
    <h2 class="text-3xl font-bold mb-8 text-center">What Our Users
Say</h2>
    <div class="grid grid-cols-1 md:grid-cols-2 gap-8">
      <div class="bg-white p-6 rounded-lg shadow-md">
        <p class="mb-4">"ZenHub has transformed my productivity! I'm
finally organized and focused."</p>
        <p class="font-bold">- John Doe, CEO</p>
      </div>
      <div class="bg-white p-6 rounded-lg shadow-md">
        <p class="mb-4">"I love the time management features. They
help me stay on track and avoid distractions."</p>
        <p class="font-bold">- Jane Smith, Designer</p>
      </div>
    </div>
  </div>
</section>
```

This code creates a section with a light gray background and displays two testimonials in a two-column grid.

5. Call to Action

Finally, let's add a strong call to action:

HTML

```
<section class="py-10">
  <div class="container mx-auto text-center">
    <h2 class="text-3xl font-bold mb-4">Ready to Unlock Your Productivity?</h2>
    <button class="bg-blue-500 hover:bg-blue-700 text-white font-bold py-3 px-6 rounded-lg">
      Download ZenHub Now
    </button>
  </div>
</section>
```

This code creates a call-to-action section with a prominent button encouraging users to download the app.

6. Running the Code

Save your landing.html file and open it in your browser. You should see a responsive landing page with a clean and modern design.

Illustrating the Interface:

Imagine a visually appealing landing page with a vibrant blue hero section featuring a large headline, a concise description of ZenHub, and a prominent "Download Now" button. Below, you see three columns showcasing the app's key features with icons and text. Further down, there's a section with testimonials from satisfied users. Finally, a centered call to action encourages visitors to download the app.

As you resize the browser window, the layout adapts seamlessly to different screen sizes, ensuring a consistent and user-friendly experience on all devices.

Key Takeaways:

- **Utility-first approach:** We used Bootstrap's utility classes to style all the elements on the page without writing any custom CSS.
- **Responsive design:** The layout adapts to different screen sizes using Bootstrap's grid system and responsive utilities.
- **Visual hierarchy:** We used font sizes, colors, and spacing to create a clear visual hierarchy and guide the user's eye.s

- **Engaging content:** The landing page features compelling headlines, concise descriptions, and testimonials to engage visitors.
- **Clear call to action:** Prominent buttons encourage users to download the app.

This project demonstrates how to effectively use Bootstrap 5's utility classes to create a stylish and responsive landing page. By mastering this approach, you can significantly speed up your development workflow and build visually appealing websites with ease.

CHAPTER 10: ADVANCED CUSTOMIZATION AND OPTIMIZATION

10.1 Working with Bootstrap 5's Source Code

Alright, let's take our Bootstrap 5 customization skills to the ultimate level: working with the source code! This is where we go behind the scenes, peek under the hood, and truly understand how Bootstrap is built. Think of it like becoming a master mechanic – you're not just driving the car; you're taking it apart, understanding its inner workings, and fine-tuning it for optimal performance.

Working with Bootstrap's source code gives you unparalleled control and flexibility. You can:

- **Customize core styles:** Modify the Sass variables, mixins, and functions that define Bootstrap's default styles.

- **Create custom builds:** Include or exclude specific components, utilities, or JavaScript plugins to create tailored versions of Bootstrap.
- **Modify existing components:** Change the HTML structure, CSS styles, or JavaScript behavior of existing components to fit your specific needs.
- **Develop new components:** Build entirely new components from scratch, leveraging Bootstrap's existing styles and utilities.
- **Contribute to the framework:** If you're feeling adventurous, you can even contribute your own code and improvements to the Bootstrap project.

1. Obtaining the Source Code

First, you'll need to obtain the Bootstrap 5 source code. You can download it from the official GitHub repository:

https://github.com/twbs/bootstrap

The source code is organized into several folders:

- **scss:** Contains the Sass files that define Bootstrap's CSS.
- **js:** Contains the JavaScript files for Bootstrap's plugins and components.
- **dist:** Contains the compiled CSS and JavaScript files that you typically include in your projects.

2. Understanding the Sass Structure

Bootstrap's CSS is built with Sass, a powerful CSS preprocessor that adds features like variables, mixins, and functions. The scss folder contains the Sass files that define Bootstrap's styles.

The main Sass files are:

- **_variables.scss:** Contains the variables that control Bootstrap's default styles, such as colors, fonts, and spacing.
- **_functions.scss:** Contains Sass functions used throughout the framework.

- **_mixins.scss:** Contains Sass mixins for reusable style blocks.
- **bootstrap.scss:** The main Sass file that imports all the other files and compiles into Bootstrap's CSS.

3. Customizing with Sass

You can customize Bootstrap's styles by modifying the Sass variables, mixins, and functions. Create a custom Sass file in your project and import Bootstrap's Sass files. Then, override the default variables or create your own mixins to modify the styles.

For example, to change the primary color, you would override the $primary variable:

SCSS

```scss
$primary: #663399; // Your custom color

@import "bootstrap/scss/bootstrap";
```

4. Creating Custom Builds

Bootstrap provides a build tool that allows you to create custom versions of the framework. You can choose which components, utilities, or JavaScript plugins to include in your build, reducing the file size and improving performance.

To use the build tool, you'll need to have Node.js and npm installed. Then, follow these steps:

1. **Navigate to the Bootstrap source code directory.**
2. **Install the dependencies:** npm install
3. **Run the build tool:** npm run dist
4. **Customize the build:** Modify the scss/custom.scss file to include or exclude specific components or utilities.
5. **Rebuild the CSS:** npm run css

5. Modifying Existing Components

You can modify the HTML structure, CSS styles, or JavaScript behavior of existing components by editing the corresponding files in the source code. This allows you to create custom variations of Bootstrap components that perfectly match your needs.

For example, you could modify the modal.js file to add custom animations or transitions to the modal component.

6. Developing New Components

You can create entirely new components from scratch by leveraging Bootstrap's existing styles and utilities. This allows you to extend Bootstrap's capabilities and build a library of custom components for your projects.

For example, you could create a new "accordion" component by combining Bootstrap's collapse plugin with custom HTML, CSS, and JavaScript.

Illustrating Source Code Customization

Imagine you want to create a unique button style that's not available in Bootstrap's default set. You can achieve this by:

1. **Creating a new Sass mixin:** Define a mixin that applies your custom button styles.
2. **Including the mixin in your custom Sass file:** Import your mixin and apply it to a new button class.

3. **Compiling your Sass:** Compile your Sass file to generate the CSS with your custom button style.

This approach allows you to extend Bootstrap's styling capabilities and create a truly personalized design system.

Experiment and Explore!

Working with Bootstrap 5's source code gives you ultimate control and flexibility over the framework. Explore the Sass structure, experiment with customizing variables and mixins, create custom builds, modify existing components, and develop your own unique components.

10.2 Advanced Sass Customization

10.2.1 Mixin Customization and Function Creation

Alright, let's dive deeper into the heart of Sass and explore how to customize existing mixins and even create our own functions! This is where we truly unlock the power and flexibility of Bootstrap 5's Sass architecture, tailoring it to our precise needs and design preferences.

Think of mixins as reusable code snippets that encapsulate a set of CSS properties. They're like templates or recipes that you can use to apply consistent styles throughout your project.

Bootstrap 5 provides a wealth of mixins for various styling purposes, such as:

- **border-radius():** Creates rounded corners.
- **box-shadow():** Adds a box shadow.
- **transition():** Creates smooth transitions between states.
- **clearfix():** Clears floats.

- **gradients():** Generates gradients.

Customizing Existing Mixins

You can customize Bootstrap's mixins by overriding their default parameters or adding your own logic. This allows you to tweak the mixin's behavior to match your specific requirements.

For example, let's say you want to modify the border-radius() mixin to create a pill-shaped border radius. You can override the $radius parameter like this:

SCSS

```scss
@use "bootstrap/scss/mixins";

.my-element {
  @include mixins.border-radius(50rem); // Create a pill shape
}
```

This code snippet calls the border-radius() mixin with a very large radius (50rem), effectively creating a pill shape.

Creating Your Own Mixins

You can also create your own mixins to encapsulate custom styles or reusable logic. This can significantly improve the organization and maintainability of your Sass code.

For example, let's say you want to create a mixin for adding a hover effect that changes the background color and text color of an element:

SCSS

```
@mixin hover-effect($hover-bg, $hover-color) {
  &:hover {
    background-color: $hover-bg;
    color: $hover-color;
  }
}
```

This mixin takes two parameters: the hover background color and the hover text color. You can then use this mixin in your Sass code like this:

SCSS

```
.my-button {
  @include hover-effect(#007bff, #fff);
}
```

This will apply the hover effect to the .my-button class, changing its background color to blue and its text color to white on hover.

Sass Functions

Sass functions are similar to mixins, but they return a value instead of generating CSS rules. They're like mini-programs that perform calculations or manipulate data within your Sass code.

Bootstrap 5 provides several built-in functions, such as:

- **color-contrast():** Calculates the contrast ratio between two colors.
- **theme-color-level():** Retrieves a color from the theme palette based on its level.
- **map-get():** Retrieves a value from a Sass map.

Creating Custom Functions

You can also create your own custom functions to encapsulate reusable logic or perform specific calculations.

For example, let's say you want to create a function that converts pixels to rems:

SCSS

```
@function px-to-rem($px) {
  @return $px / 16 + rem;
}
```

This function takes a pixel value as input and returns the equivalent value in rems. You can then use this function in your Sass code like this:

SCSS

```
.my-element {
  font-size: px-to-rem(16px); // Equivalent to 1rem
}
```

Illustrating Mixin and Function Customization

Imagine you're building a website with a unique button style that requires a specific gradient background and hover effect. You can achieve this by:

1. **Customizing the gradient() mixin:** Modify the mixin to generate the desired gradient.

2. **Creating a custom hover effect mixin:** Define a mixin that applies your custom hover styles.

3. **Applying the mixins:** Use the mixins to style your button.

This approach allows you to extend Bootstrap's styling capabilities and create a truly personalized design system.

Experiment and Explore!

Customizing mixins and creating functions are powerful techniques for advanced Sass customization. They allow you to encapsulate reusable logic, modify existing styles, and create a truly bespoke design system for your Bootstrap 5 projects.

Explore the possibilities, experiment with different mixin parameters and function logic, and discover how these techniques can enhance your workflow and empower you to create unique and expressive web designs.

10.2.2 Building Complex Themes with Sass

Alright, let's take our Sass customization skills to the next level and build complex themes for Bootstrap 5! This is where we truly unleash the power of Sass to create unique and sophisticated designs that go beyond simple color tweaks and font changes.

Think of it like this: instead of just choosing a pre-designed template, we're now architects crafting a custom-built house with intricate details, personalized layouts, and a unique style that reflects our vision.

Building complex themes with Sass involves a deeper understanding of Sass features like:

- **Variables:** Controlling the values of colors, fonts, spacing, and other design elements.
- **Mixins:** Encapsulating reusable style blocks for consistent and efficient styling.
- **Functions:** Performing calculations and manipulating values within your Sass code.

- **Nesting:** Organizing your Sass code in a structured and maintainable way.
- **Maps:** Storing and accessing collections of values for complex theming logic.
- **Control flow:** Using @if, @else, and @for statements to create dynamic styles based on conditions or loops.

1. Planning Your Theme

Before diving into code, carefully plan your theme's design:

- **Visual style:** Define the overall look and feel you want to achieve. Create a mood board or style guide to capture your vision.
- **Color palette:** Choose a harmonious set of colors that reflect your brand or project.
- **Typography:** Select appropriate font families, sizes, and weights for different elements.
- **Spacing and layout:** Determine the spacing, grid system, and layout patterns you'll use.

- **Component customization:** Identify which Bootstrap components you'll customize and how.

2. Organizing Your Sass

Structure your Sass code in a modular and organized way. Use separate files for different aspects of your theme, such as variables, mixins, and component styles. This improves maintainability and makes it easier to collaborate with others.

For example, you might create the following files:

- **_variables.scss:** Contains your custom theme variables.
- **_mixins.scss:** Contains your custom mixins.
- **_buttons.scss:** Contains styles for customizing buttons.
- **_forms.scss:** Contains styles for customizing forms.
- **theme.scss:** The main Sass file that imports all the other files.

3. Customizing Variables

Override Bootstrap's default variables in your _variables.scss file to create your unique theme. You can change colors, fonts, spacing, breakpoints, and much more.

SCSS

```
// _variables.scss

// Color palette
$primary: #663399; // Purple
$secondary: #f8f9fa; // Light gray
$body-bg: #ffffff; // White

// Font family
$font-family-sans-serif: 'Roboto', sans-serif;

// Container width
$container-max-widths: (
  sm: 540px,
  md: 720px,
  lg: 960px,
  xl: 1140px,
  xxl: 1320px
);

// ... other variables
```

4. Creating Custom Mixins

Define reusable mixins in your _mixins.scss file to encapsulate common styles or complex logic.

SCSS

```
// _mixins.scss

@mixin button-variant($bg, $color) {
  background-color: $bg;
  color: $color;
  border: none;

  &:hover {
    background-color: darken($bg, 10%);
  }
}
```

5. Customizing Components

In your component-specific Sass files (e.g., _buttons.scss), use mixins and variables to customize Bootstrap components.

SCSS

```
// _buttons.scss

.btn-primary {
  @include button-variant($primary, #fff);
}

.btn-secondary {
  @include button-variant($secondary, #343a40);
}
```

6. Leveraging Advanced Sass Features

Use advanced Sass features like maps, control flow, and nesting to create complex theming logic.

For example, you could use a Sass map to define different button styles and then use a @each loop to generate CSS classes for each style.

7. Compiling Your Sass

Compile your Sass files into a CSS file that you can include in your HTML.

Illustrating Complex Themes

Imagine a website with a dark theme that uses a unique color palette, custom gradients, and modified button styles. This theme could be achieved by:

- **Overriding Bootstrap's color variables:** Setting $body-bg to a dark color and defining a set of contrasting colors for other elements.
- **Creating custom gradient mixins:** Defining mixins that generate the desired gradients.

- **Customizing button styles:** Using mixins and variables to create unique button styles with hover effects and shadows.

Experiment and Explore!

Building complex themes with Sass allows you to create truly unique and sophisticated designs for your Bootstrap 5 projects. Explore the full potential of Sass, experiment with different techniques, and create a theme that perfectly captures your vision and elevates your web design to new heights.

10.3 Optimizing for Performance

10.3.1 Critical CSS, Code Splitting, and Lazy Loading

Alright, let's shift gears and focus on optimizing our Bootstrap 5 projects for performance! This is where we fine-tune our websites to load faster, run smoother, and provide a better user experience. Think of it like tuning up a race car – we're optimizing every component to squeeze out maximum speed and efficiency.

In the world of web development, performance is paramount. Users expect websites to load quickly and respond instantly to their interactions. A slow or sluggish website can lead to frustration, abandonment, and lost conversions.

This section will explore three powerful techniques for optimizing your Bootstrap 5 projects: critical CSS, code splitting, and lazy loading. These techniques can significantly improve your website's loading speed and overall performance.

Critical CSS: Prioritizing Above-the-Fold Content

Critical CSS is the CSS code that's essential for rendering the content that's immediately visible to the user when they first load your web page (the "above-the-fold" content). By inlining this critical CSS directly in your HTML, you can eliminate render-blocking external stylesheets and speed up the initial page load.

Think of it like serving the main course first and then bringing out the side dishes later. You satisfy the user's immediate hunger (displaying the critical content quickly) and then enhance the experience with the rest of the meal (loading the non-critical CSS).

Here's how to implement critical CSS:

1. **Identify critical CSS:** Determine the CSS rules that are necessary to style the above-the-fold content. You can use browser developer tools or online tools to help with this.

2. **Inline the critical CSS:** Copy the critical CSS and paste it directly into a <style> tag in the <head> of your HTML document.

3. **Load the remaining CSS asynchronously:** Load the rest of your CSS asynchronously using a <link> tag with the async or defer attribute. This allows the browser to render the page without waiting for the non-critical CSS to load.

Code Splitting: Breaking Down the Bundle

Code splitting is a technique that involves breaking down your JavaScript code into smaller, more manageable chunks. Instead of loading the entire JavaScript bundle at once, you can load only the code that's needed for the current page or section. This can significantly reduce the initial load time and improve performance, especially for large applications.

Think of it like packing for a trip. Instead of carrying one massive suitcase with everything you might need, you pack smaller bags with only the essentials for each leg of your journey.

Here's how to implement code splitting:

1. **Identify split points:** Determine logical points in your code where you can split it into smaller chunks. This might be based on different routes, components, or features.

2. **Use dynamic imports:** Use JavaScript's dynamic import() function to load code chunks on demand. This allows you to load code only when it's needed.

3. **Configure your build tool:** Configure your build tool (e.g., Webpack, Parcel, Rollup) to support code splitting. The build tool will generate separate bundles for each code chunk.

Lazy Loading: Delaying Non-Critical Resources

Lazy loading is a technique that delays the loading of non-critical resources, such as images or videos, until they are needed. This can further improve initial page load time and reduce bandwidth consumption.

Think of it like a buffet. You don't fill your plate with everything at once; you take what you want initially and then go back for more if needed.

Here's how to implement lazy loading:

1. **Use the loading attribute:** For images, add the loading="lazy" attribute to the <img> tag. This tells the browser to load the image only when it's about to enter the viewport.
2. **Use JavaScript libraries:** For more complex lazy loading scenarios, use JavaScript libraries like lazysizes or lozad.js. These libraries provide more advanced features and options for lazy loading various types of content.

Illustrating Performance Optimization

Imagine a website with a large hero image and several interactive components. By implementing critical CSS, code splitting, and lazy loading, you can significantly improve its performance:

- **Critical CSS:** The hero image and the initial visible content load quickly because the critical CSS is inlined in the HTML.
- **Code splitting:** The JavaScript code for interactive components is loaded only when the user interacts with them, reducing the initial bundle size.
- **Lazy loading:** Images below the fold are loaded only when they are about to enter the viewport, further reducing the initial load time.

This optimized website provides a faster and smoother user experience, leading to increased engagement and satisfaction.

Experiment and Explore!

Optimizing for performance is an essential aspect of modern web development. Experiment with critical CSS, code splitting, and lazy loading to see how they can improve your Bootstrap 5 projects. Use browser developer tools to measure your website's performance and identify areas for improvement.

By mastering these techniques, you can create high-performing websites that provide a delightful user experience.

10.3.2 Image Optimization Techniques

Alright, let's dive into the world of image optimization! Images are often the heaviest elements on a web page, and optimizing them can significantly impact your website's loading speed and performance. Think of it like packing for a hike – you want to bring the essentials, but you also want to keep your backpack as light as possible.

Optimizing images involves reducing their file size without sacrificing too much quality. This allows your web pages to load faster, consume less bandwidth, and provide a better user experience.

Here's a breakdown of essential image optimization techniques:

1. Choose the Right File Format

Selecting the appropriate file format is crucial for image optimization. Different formats have different compression algorithms and characteristics, making them suitable for various types of images.

Here are some common formats:

- **JPEG:** Ideal for photographs and images with complex colors and details. Offers good compression with some loss of quality.
- **PNG:** Suitable for images with sharp lines, text, or transparency. Offers lossless compression, preserving all image data.
- **WebP:** A modern format that provides superior compression compared to JPEG and PNG. Supports both lossy and lossless compression.
- **SVG:** A vector format ideal for icons, logos, and illustrations. Scalable without losing quality.

Choosing the right format depends on the type of image and the desired balance between file size and quality.

2. Compress Your Images

Compression is the process of reducing the file size of an image by removing redundant data or applying lossy compression algorithms. There are various tools and techniques available for compressing images:

- **Online tools:** Websites like TinyPNG, Compressor.io, and ImageOptim offer easy-to-use image compression with good results.
- **Image editing software:** Most image editing software (e.g., Photoshop, GIMP) includes built-in compression features.
- **Command-line tools:** Tools like imagemin or optipng provide more advanced compression options for automation and integration with build processes.

Experiment with different compression levels to find the optimal balance between file size and quality.

3. Resize Images Appropriately

Don't upload images that are larger than necessary. Resize your images to the dimensions they will be displayed on your web page. This avoids wasting bandwidth and storage space on unnecessarily large images.

Use image editing software or online tools to resize images before uploading them.

4. Use Responsive Images

Responsive images are images that adapt to different screen sizes and resolutions. This ensures that users on different devices receive the optimal image size, improving performance and user experience.

Here's how to implement responsive images:

- **<picture> element:** Use the <picture> element to provide different image sources for different screen sizes or resolutions.
- **srcset and sizes attributes:** Use the srcset and sizes attributes in the <img> tag to specify different image sources and their corresponding display sizes.
- **Image CDNs:** Consider using image CDNs (Content Delivery Networks) that automatically optimize and deliver images based on the user's device and network conditions.

5. Optimize Image Metadata

Image metadata includes information about the image, such as camera settings, location data, and copyright information. This metadata can add unnecessary bloat to your image files.

Use image editing software or online tools to remove or optimize image metadata.

6. Lazy Load Images

As discussed in the previous section, lazy loading can significantly improve initial page load time by delaying the loading of images until they are needed.

Use the loading="lazy" attribute or JavaScript libraries to implement lazy loading for your images.

Illustrating Image Optimization

Imagine a website with a large hero image. By applying these optimization techniques, you can significantly reduce the image's file size:

- **Choose WebP format:** Convert the image to WebP format for superior compression.

- **Compress the image:** Use an online tool or image editing software to compress the image further.
- **Resize the image:** Resize the image to the exact dimensions it will be displayed on the page.
- **Use responsive images:** Provide different image sources for different screen sizes.
- **Optimize metadata:** Remove unnecessary metadata from the image file.
- **Lazy load the image:** Delay the loading of the image until it's about to enter the viewport.

This optimized image will load much faster, improving the website's overall performance and user experience.

Experiment and Explore!

Image optimization is a crucial aspect of web performance. Experiment with different file formats, compression techniques, and responsive image solutions to find the best approach for your Bootstrap 5 projects. Use browser developer tools to analyze your website's image loading performance and identify areas for improvement.

By mastering these techniques, you can significantly reduce your website's loading times and provide a smoother and more enjoyable user experience.

10.3.3 Bootstrap 5 and Build Tools (Webpack, Parcel, Rollup)

Okay, let's explore how to supercharge your Bootstrap 5 projects with build tools! These powerful tools automate tasks, optimize your code, and streamline your development workflow. Think of them as your trusty robotic assistants, taking care of the tedious and repetitive tasks so you can focus on the creative aspects of building amazing web applications.

In the world of modern web development, build tools have become essential for managing complex projects, improving performance, and ensuring compatibility across different browsers. They can handle tasks like:

- **Bundling:** Combining multiple JavaScript and CSS files into a single file to reduce HTTP requests and improve loading times.
- **Transpiling:** Converting modern JavaScript (ES6+) code into older versions that are compatible with older browsers.
- **Minifying:** Removing unnecessary characters (whitespace, comments) from your code to reduce file size and improve performance.
- **Code splitting:** Breaking down your code into smaller chunks that can be loaded on demand, improving initial load time.
- **Module resolution:** Resolving dependencies between different modules and libraries.
- **Hot module replacement:** Automatically updating your browser when you make changes to your code, speeding up development.

Popular Build Tools

Here are some of the most popular build tools used in web development:

- **Webpack:** A powerful and highly configurable build tool with a vast ecosystem of plugins and loaders.
- **Parcel:** A zero-configuration build tool that's easy to use and requires minimal setup.
- **Rollup:** A module bundler that's particularly well-suited for libraries and applications with many dependencies.

Integrating with Bootstrap 5

You can seamlessly integrate Bootstrap 5 with any of these build tools. Here's a general overview of the process:

1. **Install the build tool:** Use npm or yarn to install the build tool of your choice.
2. **Configure the build tool:** Create a configuration file (e.g., webpack.config.js for Webpack) to specify how the

build tool should process your code. This includes defining entry points, output files, loaders, and plugins.

3. **Import Bootstrap:** Import Bootstrap's CSS and JavaScript files into your project's entry point (usually your main JavaScript file).

4. **Customize Bootstrap (optional):** If you need to customize Bootstrap's Sass variables or create custom builds, configure the build tool to process your Sass files and generate the desired CSS output.

5. **Run the build tool:** Use the build tool's command-line interface to bundle your code and generate the optimized output files.

Example: Using Webpack with Bootstrap 5

Here's a basic example of how to use Webpack with Bootstrap 5:

1. **Install Webpack:**

Bash

```
npm install webpack webpack-cli --save-dev
```

2. Create a webpack.config.js file:

JavaScript

```
const path = require('path');

module.exports = {
  entry: './src/index.js',
  output: {
    filename: 'main.js',
    path: path.resolve(__dirname, 'dist'),
  },
  module: {
    rules: [
      {
        test: /\.css$/i,
        use: ['style-loader', 'css-loader'],
      },
    ],
  },
};
```

3. Import Bootstrap in your src/index.js file:

JavaScript

```
import 'bootstrap/dist/css/bootstrap.min.css';
import 'bootstrap/dist/js/bootstrap.bundle.min.js';

// Your application code here...
```

4. Run Webpack:

Bash

```
npx webpack
```

This will bundle your code and generate the main.js file in the dist folder, including Bootstrap's CSS and JavaScript.

Benefits of Using Build Tools

Build tools offer several benefits for your Bootstrap 5 projects:

- **Improved performance:** Bundling, minification, and code splitting can significantly improve your website's loading speed and performance.
- **Enhanced development workflow:** Build tools automate tasks, streamline your workflow, and provide features like hot module replacement for faster development.
- **Modular code:** Build tools enable you to organize your code into modules, making it more maintainable and scalable.
- **Compatibility:** Build tools can handle transpiling your code to ensure compatibility with older browsers.

- **Ecosystem:** Popular build tools have extensive ecosystems with plugins and loaders that extend their functionality.

10.4 Accessibility Considerations

Alright, let's shift our focus to an essential aspect of web development: **accessibility**. This is about making our websites usable by everyone, including people with disabilities. Think of it like designing a building with ramps, elevators, and Braille signage – it ensures that everyone can access and navigate the space comfortably.

In the context of web development, accessibility means that people with visual, auditory, motor, or cognitive disabilities can perceive, understand, navigate, and interact with your website. It's not just about complying with regulations; it's about creating an inclusive online experience for all.

Bootstrap 5 provides a solid foundation for building accessible websites. It incorporates many accessibility features and best practices out of the box. However, it's crucial to be mindful of accessibility considerations throughout your development process.

Here are some key areas to focus on:

1. Semantic HTML

Use semantic HTML5 elements to structure your content and provide meaning to assistive technologies like screen readers. For example, use <nav> for navigation, <article> for main content, <aside> for sidebars, and <h1> to <h6> for headings.

Bootstrap's components are built with semantic HTML, but it's important to use them correctly and maintain a logical structure in your code.

2. ARIA Attributes

ARIA (Accessible Rich Internet Applications) attributes provide additional information to assistive technologies about the roles, states, and properties of your web page elements.

Bootstrap uses ARIA attributes in many of its components, such as modals, dropdowns, and carousels. You can also add ARIA attributes to your custom components to enhance their accessibility.

Some common ARIA attributes include:

- aria-label: Provides a label for an element that doesn't have a visible label.
- aria-expanded: Indicates whether an element is expanded or collapsed.
- aria-hidden: Indicates whether an element is visible or hidden to assistive technologies.
- aria-disabled: Indicates whether an element is disabled.
- role: Defines the role of an element (e.g., button, navigation, alert).

3. Keyboard Navigation

Ensure that all interactive elements on your website can be accessed and operated using the keyboard alone. This is crucial for users who cannot use a mouse or have limited motor skills.

Bootstrap's components are generally keyboard accessible, but it's important to test your website thoroughly to ensure that all interactive elements can be navigated and operated using the Tab key and other keyboard commands.

4. Color Contrast

Sufficient color contrast between text and background is essential for users with low vision or color blindness. Use a contrast checking tool to ensure that your color combinations meet accessibility guidelines (WCAG).

Bootstrap provides a set of color palettes with good contrast, but it's important to be mindful of color contrast when customizing styles or adding your own content.

5. Alternative Text for Images

Provide alternative text (alt text) for all images on your website. This text describes the image to users who cannot see it, such as those using screen readers.

Use the alt attribute in the <img> tag to provide descriptive alt text.

6. Focus Management

Clearly indicate which element has focus when navigating with the keyboard. This helps users understand where they are on the page and what element they are interacting with.

Bootstrap provides default focus styles for interactive elements, but you can customize them to match your design preferences while ensuring they remain visible and distinguishable.

7. Accessible Forms

Design forms that are accessible to users with disabilities. This includes:

- Providing labels for all input fields.
- Using ARIA attributes to provide additional information about form controls.
- Grouping related fields and providing clear instructions.
- Providing error messages that are easy to understand and locate.

Bootstrap's form components are designed with accessibility in mind, but it's essential to follow best practices when creating and styling your forms.

8. Testing and Validation

Test your website with assistive technologies like screen readers and keyboard navigation to ensure it's accessible to users with disabilities. Use online accessibility testing tools to identify potential issues and validate your code against accessibility guidelines.

Illustrating Accessibility

Imagine a website with a modal window. The modal has a clear heading, ARIA attributes that indicate its role and state, and can be navigated and closed using the keyboard. The modal's content has sufficient color contrast and includes alternative text for any images.

This accessible modal provides a positive experience for all users, regardless of their abilities.

Experiment and Explore!

Accessibility is an ongoing process. Continuously test your website, learn about new accessibility guidelines and techniques, and strive to create an inclusive online experience for everyone.

By incorporating accessibility considerations into your Bootstrap 5 projects, you can create websites that are not only visually appealing and functional but also usable by the widest possible audience.

10.5 Project: Building a Complex Dashboard with Custom Components

Alright, let's combine everything we've learned and build a complex dashboard with custom Bootstrap 5 components! This project will showcase how to leverage advanced Sass customization, JavaScript interactivity, and performance optimization techniques to create a powerful and engaging data visualization tool.

Think of it like this: we're not just building a simple dashboard; we're crafting a sophisticated control panel for a spaceship, with intricate displays, real-time data updates, and custom controls that respond to the pilot's every command.

Our dashboard will visualize data for a fictional online learning platform called "EduSpark." It will display key metrics like student enrollment, course completion rates, and engagement levels.

1. Planning the Dashboard

Before writing any code, let's plan the structure and features:

- **Layout:** A three-column layout with a sidebar on the left, a main content area in the center, and a right panel for user-specific information.
- **Custom Components:**
    - **Progress Circle:** A circular progress bar to visualize course completion rates.
    - **Engagement Meter:** A custom gauge component to display student engagement levels.
    - **Data Table:** An interactive table to display detailed student data with sorting and filtering capabilities.
- **Interactive Charts:**
    - **Line chart:** To show enrollment trends over time.
    - **Bar chart:** To compare course completion rates across different categories.

- **Filters:** Allow users to filter data by date range, course category, and student demographics.

2. Building the Foundation

Create a new HTML file (dashboard.html) and set up the basic structure with Bootstrap 5's CSS and JavaScript files. Use the grid system to create the three-column layout.

3. Creating Custom Components

- **Progress Circle:**

HTML

```
<div class="progress-circle">
  <div class="progress-circle-value">75%</div>
  <svg>
    <circle cx="50" cy="50" r="40"></circle>
    <circle cx="50" cy="50" r="40" style="stroke-
dasharray: 251.2;"></circle>
  </svg>
</div>
```

CSS

```
.progress-circle {
  position: relative;
  width: 100px;
  height: 100px;

  svg {
    width: 100%;
```

```
    height: 100%;
    transform: rotate(-90deg);
  }

  circle {
    fill: none;
    stroke-width: 10;
    stroke-linecap: round;
  }

  circle:first-of-type {
    stroke: #e9ecef;
  }

  circle:last-of-type {
    stroke: #007bff;
    stroke-dasharray: 0;
    transition: stroke-dasharray 0.3s ease;
  }

  .progress-circle-value {
    position: absolute;
    top: 50%;
    left: 50%;
    transform: translate(-50%, -50%);
    font-size: 1.2rem;
    font-weight: bold;
  }
}
```

- **Engagement Meter:** Use a similar approach with SVG or a charting library to create a custom gauge.
- **Data Table:** Enhance a standard HTML table with JavaScript for sorting and filtering functionality.

4. Integrating Interactive Charts

Use Chart.js or another charting library to create interactive line and bar charts. Bind the chart data to variables that can be updated based on user filter selections.

5. Implementing Filters

Add form controls (dropdowns, date pickers) to the sidebar to allow users to filter the data. Use JavaScript to update the chart data and custom component values based on the selected filters.

6. Advanced Sass Customization

Create a custom Sass file to override Bootstrap variables, define custom mixins, and style your components. Use Sass functions to calculate values dynamically and create complex theming logic.

7. Optimizing for Performance

- **Critical CSS:** Inline the critical CSS for above-the-fold content to improve initial load time.

- **Code splitting:** Break down your JavaScript code into smaller chunks to reduce the initial bundle size.
- **Lazy loading:** Delay the loading of images and other non-critical resources.
- **Image optimization:** Optimize your images to reduce their file size.

8. Illustrating the Dashboard

Imagine a sleek dashboard with a dark theme and vibrant accent colors. The progress circles vividly display course completion rates, while the engagement meters provide an intuitive visualization of student activity. The interactive charts dynamically update based on filter selections, and the data table allows users to drill down into specific student details.

This complex dashboard provides a powerful and engaging tool for monitoring and analyzing data, showcasing the flexibility and customization capabilities of Bootstrap 5.

Experiment and Explore!

Building complex dashboards with custom components is a challenging but rewarding endeavor. It allows you to create truly unique and tailored data visualization tools that meet your specific needs.

Experiment with different component designs, chart types, and interactive features. Leverage the full power of Sass and JavaScript to customize Bootstrap 5 and create a dashboard that's both visually appealing and functionally rich.

CHAPTER 11: ADVANCED BOOTSTRAP 5 TECHNIQUES

11.1 Working with the Bootstrap 5 Source Code:

11.1.1 Modifying Core Files and Building Custom Distributions

Alright, let's dive deep into the engine room of Bootstrap 5 and explore how to modify its core files and build custom distributions! This is where we transcend being mere users of the framework and become architects, shaping Bootstrap to our will and creating truly bespoke versions tailored to our specific needs.

Think of it like this: instead of just living in a pre-built house, we're now taking on the role of builders, modifying the blueprints, choosing custom materials, and constructing a unique dwelling that perfectly reflects our vision.

Working with Bootstrap's source code gives us unparalleled control and flexibility. We can:

- **Customize core styles:** Modify the Sass variables, mixins, and functions that define Bootstrap's default look and feel.
- **Create custom builds:** Include or exclude specific components, utilities, or JavaScript plugins to optimize for performance and reduce file size.
- **Modify existing components:** Change the HTML structure, CSS styles, or JavaScript behavior of existing components to match our exact requirements.

1. Obtaining the Source Code

First, we need the Bootstrap 5 source files. Download them from the official GitHub repository:

https://github.com/twbs/bootstrap

The source code is organized into several folders:

- **scss:** Contains the Sass files that define Bootstrap's CSS.

- **js:** Contains the JavaScript files for Bootstrap's plugins and components.
- **dist:** Contains the compiled CSS and JavaScript files (what you typically use in your projects).

2. Understanding the Sass Structure

Bootstrap's CSS is built with Sass, a powerful CSS preprocessor. The scss folder holds the Sass files that define Bootstrap's styles.

The key Sass files are:

- **_variables.scss:** Contains variables controlling Bootstrap's default styles (colors, fonts, spacing).
- **_functions.scss:** Contains Sass functions used throughout the framework.
- **_mixins.scss:** Contains Sass mixins for reusable style blocks.
- **bootstrap.scss:** The main Sass file that imports all others and compiles into Bootstrap's CSS.

3. Modifying Core Files

We can customize Bootstrap by directly modifying the Sass files in the scss folder. For example, to change the primary color, we can edit _variables.scss and modify the $primary variable:

```scss
// _variables.scss
$primary: #663399; // Our custom purple
```

This change will affect all components and utilities that use the $primary variable.

4. Building Custom Distributions

Bootstrap provides a build tool that lets us create custom versions of the framework. We can choose which components, utilities, or JavaScript plugins to include, optimizing for performance and reducing file size.

To use the build tool, you'll need Node.js and npm installed. Then, follow these steps:

1. **Navigate to the Bootstrap source code directory.**
2. **Install the dependencies:** npm install
3. **Run the build tool:** npm run dist (This creates a default distribution in the dist folder)
4. **Customize the build:** Modify the scss/custom.scss file to include or exclude specific components or utilities. You can comment out @import statements for components you don't need.
5. **Rebuild the CSS:** npm run css (This generates a new bootstrap.css file based on your customizations)

5. Modifying Existing Components

We can modify existing components by editing the corresponding files in the scss and js folders. For example, to change the default styles of the modal component, we can edit scss/_modal.scss. To modify its JavaScript behavior, we can edit js/src/modal.js.

Caution: Modifying core files requires careful consideration. It can make updating to newer Bootstrap versions more challenging. Always back up your original files and thoroughly test your changes.

Illustrating Customization

Imagine you want to create a lightweight version of Bootstrap that only includes the grid system and a few essential components (buttons, forms, alerts). You can achieve this by:

1. **Downloading the source code.**
2. **Modifying scss/custom.scss:** Comment out the @import statements for the components you don't need.
3. **Rebuilding the CSS:** Run npm run css to generate a customized bootstrap.css file.

This process creates a smaller and more efficient version of Bootstrap tailored to your specific needs.

11.2 Creating Custom Bootstrap 5 Builds

11.2.1 Including/Excluding Specific Components and Features

Alright, let's master the art of creating custom Bootstrap 5 builds! This is where we become the architects of our own framework, hand-picking the components, utilities, and JavaScript plugins we need, and discarding the rest. Think of it like ordering a bespoke suit – you choose the fabric, the cut, the buttons, and every detail to create a perfect fit.

Creating custom builds offers several benefits:

- **Reduced file size:** By including only the components and features you need, you can significantly reduce the size of your CSS and JavaScript files, leading to faster loading times and improved performance.
- **Improved performance:** Smaller file sizes translate to faster downloads and less work for the browser, resulting in a smoother user experience.

- **Reduced complexity:** A custom build with only the necessary components can simplify your development process and make your code easier to manage.
- **Enhanced maintainability:** A streamlined codebase with fewer dependencies is easier to maintain and update.

1. The custom.scss File

The key to creating custom Bootstrap 5 builds lies in the scss/custom.scss file within the Bootstrap source code. This file acts as the entry point for your custom CSS.

By default, custom.scss imports all of Bootstrap's components, utilities, and JavaScript plugins. To create a custom build, you can selectively comment out or remove the @import statements for the components and features you don't need.

For example, if you only need the grid system, buttons, and forms, your custom.scss file might look like this:

SCSS

```
// scss/custom.scss

// Core variables and mixins
@import "functions";
@import "variables";
@import "mixins";
@import "root";
@import "reboot";
@import "type";
@import "images";
@import "containers";
@import "grid";

// Components you need
@import "buttons";
@import "forms";

// ... other imports you might need
```

Notice that we've commented out the imports for components like alerts, badges, modal, etc.

2. Building the Custom CSS

Once you've customized the custom.scss file, you need to rebuild the CSS to generate your custom Bootstrap build. Here's how:

1. **Navigate to the Bootstrap source code directory.**
2. **Install the dependencies (if you haven't already):** npm install
3. **Run the build tool:** npm run css

This will generate a new bootstrap.css file in the dist/css folder. This file will only contain the styles for the components and features you included in your custom.scss file.

3. Including the Custom Build in Your Project

Now, you can include this custom bootstrap.css file in your HTML project instead of the default bootstrap.css file. This will ensure that you're only loading the necessary styles, reducing file size and improving performance.

4. Customizing JavaScript

If you need to customize the JavaScript plugins included in your build, you can follow a similar process:

1. **Modify the js/src/index.js file:** Comment out or remove the imports for the plugins you don't need.

2. **Rebuild the JavaScript:** Run npm run js to generate a customized bootstrap.bundle.js file.

5. Advanced Customization

For more advanced customization, you can:

- **Create multiple custom builds:** Create different builds for different sections or pages of your website, optimizing each build for its specific needs.
- **Use a build tool like Webpack:** Integrate Bootstrap's source code with a build tool like Webpack to automate the build process and further optimize your code.

Illustrating Custom Builds

Imagine you're building a landing page that only requires the grid system, buttons, and forms. By creating a custom Bootstrap build with only these components, you can significantly reduce the CSS file size, resulting in faster loading times and a better user experience.

11.3 Building Advanced Interactive Components

11.3.1 JavaScript Animations and Transitions

Alright, let's elevate our interactive components with the magic of JavaScript animations and transitions! This is where we breathe life into our user interfaces, creating dynamic and engaging experiences that captivate and delight users. Think of it like adding choreography to a stage performance – we're not just presenting static elements; we're orchestrating fluid movements and captivating transitions that enhance the storytelling.

JavaScript animations allow us to manipulate the styles and properties of HTML elements over time, creating effects like movement, fading, scaling, and transformations. Transitions, on the other hand, provide a way to smoothly animate changes to CSS properties, creating a more visually appealing and polished experience.

1. CSS Transitions

CSS transitions provide a simple and efficient way to animate changes to CSS properties. You define the properties you want to animate, the duration of the animation, and the timing function (e.g., ease, linear, ease-in-out) to control the animation's speed and flow.

Here's an example of a CSS transition that smoothly animates the background color of a button on hover:

CSS

```
.btn-transition {
  transition: background-color 0.3s ease;
}

.btn-transition:hover {
  background-color: #007bff;
}
```

In this code:

- `transition: background-color 0.3s ease;` defines the transition property (`background-color`), the duration (`0.3s`), and the timing function (`ease`).

When the user hovers over the button, the background color will smoothly transition to blue over 0.3 seconds with an ease timing function.

2. JavaScript Animations

For more complex animations or dynamic effects that require precise control, we can use JavaScript. JavaScript provides various APIs for creating animations, such as:

- **animate() method:** Allows you to animate CSS properties of an element by defining keyframes and timing options.
- **requestAnimationFrame() API:** Provides a more efficient way to create animations by synchronizing with the browser's refresh rate.
- **Third-party libraries:** Libraries like GSAP (GreenSock Animation Platform) offer powerful animation capabilities and advanced features.

Here's a simple example of using JavaScript's animate() method to move an element:

JavaScript

```
const myElement = document.getElementById('my-
element');

myElement.animate([
  { transform: 'translateX(0)' },
  { transform: 'translateX(100px)' }
], {
  duration: 1000,
  easing: 'ease-out',
  fill: 'forwards'
});
```

This code animates the transform property of the element with ID my-element, moving it 100 pixels to the right over 1 second with an ease-out timing function.

3. Integrating with Bootstrap 5

You can seamlessly integrate JavaScript animations and transitions with your Bootstrap 5 components. Here are some examples:

- **Animated Modals:** Add smooth transitions to the modal's appearance and disappearance.
- **Dynamic Dropdowns:** Animate the opening and closing of dropdown menus.

- **Interactive Carousels:** Create custom carousel animations with transitions and effects.
- **Hover Effects:** Add subtle animations to buttons, cards, or other elements on hover.

4. Illustrating Advanced Interactions

Imagine a custom dropdown component that smoothly expands and collapses its menu with a subtle bounce effect. This could be achieved by combining CSS transitions for the initial expansion and JavaScript animations for the bounce effect.

11.3.2 Microinteractions and User Experience Enhancements

Alright, let's zoom in on the tiny details that make a big difference: **microinteractions**. These subtle animations, transitions, and visual cues might seem insignificant on their own, but they play a crucial role in creating delightful and engaging user experiences. Think of them as the subtle gestures and expressions in a conversation – they add depth, personality, and emotional connection to the interaction.

Microinteractions are those small, contained moments within a user interface that provide feedback, guide the user, or enhance the overall experience. They can be as simple as a button changing color on hover or as complex as a loading animation that transforms into a checkmark upon completion.

Why Microinteractions Matter

Microinteractions might seem like minor details, but they have a significant impact on user experience:

- **Provide feedback:** They acknowledge user actions and provide immediate feedback, reassuring users that the system is responding.

- **Guide the user:** They subtly guide users through the interface, highlighting important elements or providing visual cues.
- **Prevent errors:** They can prevent errors by confirming actions or providing warnings.
- **Add delight:** Well-designed microinteractions can add a touch of delight and personality to the user experience, making it more enjoyable and memorable.

Examples of Microinteractions

Here are some examples of microinteractions you might encounter on the web:

- **Hover effects:** A button changing color or size on hover.
- **Loading animations:** A spinning loader or progress bar indicating that something is loading.
- **Success messages:** A green checkmark or a message confirming a successful action.

- **Error messages:** A red "x" or a message indicating an error.
- **Animated transitions:** Smooth transitions between different states or views.
- **Scroll triggers:** Animations or effects that are triggered when the user scrolls.
- **Sound effects:** Subtle sounds that accompany interactions, like a click or a notification.

Implementing Microinteractions with Bootstrap 5

Bootstrap 5 provides a solid foundation for implementing microinteractions. Here's how you can leverage its features:

- **CSS transitions:** Use CSS transitions to create smooth animations for hover effects, state changes, and other interactions.
- **JavaScript animations:** Use JavaScript to create more complex animations or dynamic effects.

- **Utilities:** Bootstrap's utility classes can be used to quickly add hover effects, transitions, and other visual cues.
- **Components:** Many Bootstrap components, like modals and dropdowns, already include built-in microinteractions.

Best Practices for Microinteractions

- **Keep it subtle:** Microinteractions should be subtle and not distract from the main content or functionality.
- **Provide context:** Microinteractions should provide context and meaning to the user.
- **Use appropriate timing:** The timing and duration of microinteractions should feel natural and intuitive.
- **Be consistent:** Maintain consistency in your microinteractions throughout your website or application.

- **Test and iterate:** Test your microinteractions with users to ensure they are effective and enhance the overall experience.

Illustrating Microinteractions

Imagine a form with an input field. When the user focuses on the field, a subtle animation highlights the field, providing visual feedback and guiding the user's attention. When the user enters invalid data, a small red "x" appears next to the field, providing immediate feedback and preventing errors.

These microinteractions enhance the user experience by providing clear feedback and guidance, making the form more intuitive and user-friendly.

Experiment and Explore!

Microinteractions are a powerful tool for enhancing user experience. Experiment with different animation techniques, explore Bootstrap's capabilities, and discover how you can add those subtle details that make your web applications more engaging and delightful.

By mastering the art of microinteractions, you can create truly polished and user-centric designs that leave a lasting positive impression.

1.4 Accessibility and Internationalization

11.4.1 ARIA Attributes and Accessibility Best Practices

Alright, let's delve deeper into accessibility and explore the powerful role of ARIA attributes in creating inclusive web experiences with Bootstrap 5. ARIA, which stands for Accessible Rich Internet Applications, is a set of attributes that enhance the accessibility of web content, especially for users who rely on assistive technologies like screen readers.

Think of ARIA attributes as labels and instructions that provide additional context and meaning to web page elements. They help assistive technologies understand the purpose and functionality of elements that might not be inherently clear from the HTML structure alone.

Key ARIA Concepts

- **Roles:** Define the role of an element (e.g., button, navigation, alert).
- **States:** Describe the current state of an element (e.g., checked, disabled, expanded).

- **Properties:** Provide additional information about an element (e.g., aria-label, aria-describedby).

Using ARIA Attributes with Bootstrap 5

Bootstrap 5 incorporates ARIA attributes in many of its components to enhance their accessibility. For example:

- **Modals:** Use aria-modal="true" to indicate that an element is a modal dialog.
- **Dropdowns:** Use aria-expanded="true/false" to indicate whether a dropdown menu is expanded or collapsed.
- **Carousels:** Use aria-hidden="true/false" to indicate whether a carousel slide is currently visible.

You can also add ARIA attributes to your custom components to improve their accessibility.

Accessibility Best Practices with Bootstrap 5

Beyond ARIA attributes, here are some essential accessibility best practices to keep in mind when working with Bootstrap 5:

- **Semantic HTML:** Use semantic HTML5 elements to structure your content and provide meaning to assistive technologies.
- **Keyboard Navigation:** Ensure that all interactive elements can be accessed and operated using the keyboard alone.
- **Color Contrast:** Maintain sufficient color contrast between text and background.
- **Alternative Text for Images:** Provide alternative text (alt text) for all images.
- **Focus Management:** Clearly indicate which element has focus when navigating with the keyboard.
- **Accessible Forms:** Design forms that are accessible to users with disabilities, including clear labels, ARIA attributes, and error messages.
- **Testing and Validation:** Test your website with assistive technologies and online accessibility testing tools.

Example: Adding ARIA Attributes to a Custom Dropdown

Let's say you've created a custom dropdown component. You can enhance its accessibility by adding ARIA attributes:

HTML

```html
<div class="custom-dropdown" role="combobox" aria-expanded="false">
  <button class="custom-dropdown-toggle" aria-haspopup="listbox">
    Dropdown
  </button>
  <ul class="custom-dropdown-menu" aria-
labelledby="dropdownMenuButton">
    <li><a class="dropdown-item" href="#">Action</a></li>
    <li><a class="dropdown-item" href="#">Another action</a></li>
  </ul>
</div>
```

In this code:

- role="combobox" indicates that the element is a combobox (a combination of a text input and a dropdown list).
- aria-expanded="false" indicates that the dropdown menu is initially collapsed.
- aria-haspopup="listbox" indicates that the button triggers a popup listbox.

- aria-labelledby="dropdownMenuButton" associates the menu with the button that controls it.

Illustrating Accessibility with ARIA

Imagine a user with a screen reader navigating your website. When they encounter a modal window, the screen reader announces that it's a modal dialog, thanks to the aria-modal="true" attribute. The user can then use the keyboard to navigate the modal's content and interact with its elements.

This example demonstrates how ARIA attributes can significantly improve the accessibility of your web components and make your website more inclusive for users with disabilities.

11.4.2 Internationalization and Localization

Alright, let's broaden our horizons and explore the world of **internationalization and localization**! This is about making our Bootstrap 5 projects accessible and user-friendly for people across different cultures, languages, and regions. Think of it like translating a book into different languages and adapting it to different cultural contexts – it ensures that the story resonates with readers worldwide.

In web development, internationalization (often abbreviated as i18n) is the process of designing and developing your website so that it can be easily adapted to different languages and regions without requiring significant engineering changes. Localization (l10n), on the other hand, is the process of adapting your website for a specific target market, including translating text, formatting dates and numbers, and using appropriate cultural conventions.

Why Internationalization and Localization Matter

In today's interconnected world, reaching a global audience is crucial for many businesses and organizations. Internationalization and localization can help you:

- **Expand your reach:** Make your website accessible to users in different countries and regions.
- **Increase engagement:** Provide a more personalized and culturally relevant experience for users.

- **Improve user satisfaction:** Make your website easier to use and understand for people from diverse backgrounds.
- **Boost conversions:** Increase sales and conversions by catering to a wider audience.

Internationalization Best Practices

Here are some key considerations for internationalizing your Bootstrap 5 projects:

- **Use UTF-8 encoding:** Ensure your HTML files use UTF-8 encoding to support a wide range of characters and languages.
- **Separate content from code:** Store text content in separate files or databases so it can be easily translated.
- **Use locale-specific formatting:** Use appropriate formatting for dates, numbers, and currencies based on the user's locale.

- **Consider right-to-left languages:** Design your layout to support right-to-left languages like Arabic or Hebrew.
- **Provide language selection:** Allow users to choose their preferred language.

Localization with Bootstrap 5

Bootstrap 5 doesn't provide built-in localization features, but it can be easily integrated with localization libraries and tools. Here's a general approach:

1. **Choose a localization library:** Select a JavaScript library that provides localization features, such as:
    - **i18next:** A popular internationalization framework with comprehensive features.
    - **FormatJS:** A modular collection of JavaScript libraries for internationalization.
    - **Globalize:** A JavaScript library for internationalization and localization.

2. **Prepare your content for translation:** Extract text content from your HTML and store it in separate files or databases in a format that can be easily translated (e.g., JSON, YAML).

3. **Translate your content:** Use a translation service or manually translate your content into the target languages.

4. **Implement localization logic:** Use the localization library to load the appropriate translations based on the user's locale and dynamically update the UI.

Example: Using i18next with Bootstrap 5

Here's a basic example of how to use i18next with Bootstrap 5 to translate a button's text:

JavaScript

```
// Initialize i18next
i18next.init({
  lng: 'en', // Default language
  resources: {
    en: {
      translation: {
        'button-text': 'Click me'
      }
    },
    es: {
      translation: {
        'button-text': 'Haz clic en mí'
      }
    }
  }
});

// Translate the button text
const buttonText = i18next.t('button-text');

// Render the button
<button type="button" class="btn btn-primary">
  {buttonText}
</button>
```

This code initializes i18next with English and Spanish translations. It then retrieves the translated text for "button-text" based on the current language and renders the button with the translated text.

Experiment and Explore!

Internationalization and localization are crucial for creating truly global web experiences. Explore different localization libraries, learn about best practices for handling different languages and cultures, and discover how you can make your Bootstrap 5 projects accessible and engaging for users worldwide.

By embracing these techniques, you can break down language barriers and create websites that resonate with a diverse and global audience.

11.5 Integrating with CSS-in-JS Solutions

11.5.1 Styled-Components and Emotion

Alright, let's explore a modern approach to styling React components: **CSS-in-JS**! This technique, popularized by libraries like Styled-Components and Emotion, challenges the traditional separation of CSS and JavaScript, offering a more dynamic and component-centric way to style your React applications.

Think of traditional CSS as a separate wardrobe for your web page. You have different styles defined in external files, and you apply them to your HTML elements using classes. CSS-in-JS, on the other hand, is like having a built-in closet in each room of your house. Each component has its own dedicated styling space, making it more organized and self-contained.

With CSS-in-JS, you write your styles in JavaScript using tagged template literals or style objects. This allows you to:

- **Co-locate styles with components:** Keep your styles close to the components they affect, improving code organization and maintainability.

- **Dynamic styling:** Apply styles dynamically based on props, state, or theme variables.
- **Scoped styles:** Prevent style conflicts by automatically scoping styles to specific components.
- **Improved developer experience:** Leverage JavaScript features like variables, functions, and conditional logic within your styles.

Styled-Components

Styled-Components is a popular CSS-in-JS library that allows you to style your components using tagged template literals. It emphasizes a more "component-driven" styling approach, encapsulating all the CSS logic within the component itself.

Here's an example of styling a button with Styled-Components:

JavaScript

```
import styled from 'styled-components';

const Button = styled.button`
  background-color: #28a745;
  border: none;
  color: white;
  padding: 10px 20px;
  border-radius: 5px;
  cursor: pointer;

  &:hover {
    background-color: #218838;
  }
`;
```

This code creates a styled component called Button that encapsulates all the CSS styles within the template literal. You can then use this component like any other React component:

JavaScript

```
<Button>Click me</Button>
```

Emotion

Emotion is another powerful CSS-in-JS library that offers a more flexible approach. You can use both styled components and raw CSS with the css prop.

Here's an example of styling a div with Emotion:

JavaScript

```
import { css } from '@emotion/react';

const myStyle = css`
  color: #007bff;
  font-size: 1.2rem;
`;

<div css={myStyle}>This is a styled div.</div>
```

This code defines a style object using the css prop and applies it to the div.

Integrating with Bootstrap 5

You can seamlessly integrate Styled-Components or Emotion with your Bootstrap 5 projects. Here's how:

1. **Install the library:** Use npm or yarn to install Styled-Components or Emotion.
2. **Import Bootstrap's CSS:** Import Bootstrap's CSS into your project's entry point (usually your main JavaScript file).
3. **Style your components:** Use Styled-Components or Emotion to style your React components, leveraging

Bootstrap's utility classes or creating your own custom styles.

4. **Wrap Bootstrap components:** If you need to customize Bootstrap components, you can wrap them within styled components or use the css prop to apply custom styles.

Example: Customizing a Bootstrap Button with Styled-Components

JavaScript

```
import styled from 'styled-components';

const StyledButton = styled.button`
  /* Use Bootstrap's button styles as a base */
  ${({ theme }) => theme.bootstrap.btn};
  ${({ theme }) => theme.bootstrap['btn-primary']};

  /* Add custom styles */
  border-radius: 20px;
  font-weight: bold;
`;
```

This code creates a styled component called StyledButton that extends Bootstrap's btn and btn-primary styles and adds custom styles for rounded corners and bold text.

Illustrating CSS-in-JS

Imagine a React component that displays a list of products. Each product card is styled using Styled-Components, with dynamic styles based on the product's category and availability. This allows you to create a visually rich and interactive product display with ease.

11.6 Project: Building a Custom Dropdown Component with Advanced Accessibility Features

Alright, let's combine our knowledge of Bootstrap 5, JavaScript, and accessibility to build a custom dropdown component with advanced accessibility features! This project will demonstrate how to create an inclusive and user-friendly dropdown that goes beyond Bootstrap's default dropdown component, catering to users with various needs and preferences.

Think of it like designing a universal remote control that everyone can use comfortably, regardless of their physical abilities or how they interact with technology.

Our custom dropdown will have the following features:

- **Keyboard navigation:** Users can navigate the dropdown options using arrow keys, Enter, and Esc keys.

- **ARIA attributes:** Appropriate ARIA attributes will be used to provide context and information to assistive technologies.
- **Focus management:** The dropdown will clearly indicate which element has focus, especially for keyboard users.
- **Customizable styling:** The dropdown's appearance can be easily customized with CSS.
- **Touch support:** The dropdown will work seamlessly on touch devices.

1. HTML Structure

Let's start with the HTML structure for our custom dropdown:

HTML

```
<div class="custom-dropdown" role="combobox" aria-expanded="false">
  <button
    id="dropdown-button"
    class="custom-dropdown-toggle"
    aria-haspopup="listbox"
    aria-controls="dropdown-menu"
  >
    Select an option
  </button>
  <ul
    id="dropdown-menu"
    class="custom-dropdown-menu"
```

```
    aria-labelledby="dropdown-button"
    hidden
  >
    <li role="option" tabindex="0">Option 1</li>
    <li role="option" tabindex="0">Option 2</li>
    <li role="option" tabindex="0">Option 3</li>
  </ul>
</div>
```

In this structure:

- **role="combobox":** Indicates that the element is a combobox widget.
- **aria-expanded="false":** Indicates whether the dropdown menu is expanded or collapsed.
- **aria-haspopup="listbox":** Indicates that the button triggers a popup listbox.
- **aria-controls="dropdown-menu":** Specifies the ID of the element controlled by the button.
- **aria-labelledby="dropdown-button":** Associates the menu with the button that controls it.
- **role="option":** Indicates that each list item is an option in the dropdown.

- **tabindex="0":** Makes the options focusable with the keyboard.

2. CSS Styling

Next, let's add some CSS to style our dropdown:

CSS

```
.custom-dropdown-toggle {
  /* Style the button */
}

.custom-dropdown-menu {
  display: none; /* Initially hidden */
  position: absolute;
  background-color: #fff;
  box-shadow: 0 2px 5px rgba(0, 0, 0, 0.15);
  z-index: 1000; /* Ensure it appears above other elements */
}

.custom-dropdown[aria-expanded="true"] .custom-dropdown-menu {
  display: block; /* Show the menu when expanded */
}

.custom-dropdown-menu li:focus {
  background-color: #f0f0f5; /* Highlight focused option */
  outline: none;
}
```

This CSS provides basic styling for the dropdown button and menu, including a hover effect and focus state for the options.

3. JavaScript Functionality

Now, let's add the JavaScript to handle keyboard navigation, focus management, and ARIA attributes:

JavaScript

```
const dropdownToggle = document.querySelector('.custom-
dropdown-toggle');
const dropdownMenu = document.querySelector('.custom-
dropdown-menu');
const dropdownOptions = document.querySelectorAll('.custom-
dropdown-menu li');

dropdownToggle.addEventListener('click', () => {
  const expanded = dropdownToggle.getAttribute('aria-
expanded') === 'true';
  dropdownToggle.setAttribute('aria-expanded', !expanded);
  dropdownMenu.hidden = expanded;
});

// Keyboard navigation
let currentFocus = -1;

dropdownToggle.addEventListener('keydown', (event) => {
  if (event.key === 'ArrowDown' || event.key === ' ') {
    event.preventDefault();
    dropdownMenu.hidden = false;
    dropdownToggle.setAttribute('aria-expanded', true);
    currentFocus++;
    if (currentFocus >= dropdownOptions.length) currentFocus
= 0;
    dropdownOptions[currentFocus].focus();
  }
});

dropdownMenu.addEventListener('keydown', (event) => {
  if (event.key === 'ArrowDown') {
    event.preventDefault();
    currentFocus++;
    if (currentFocus >= dropdownOptions.length) currentFocus
= 0;
    dropdownOptions[currentFocus].focus();
```

```
  } else if (event.key === 'ArrowUp') {
    event.preventDefault();
    currentFocus--;
    if (currentFocus < 0) currentFocus =
dropdownOptions.length - 1;
    dropdownOptions[currentFocus].focus();
  } else if (event.key === 'Escape') {
    hideMenu();
  } else if (event.key === 'Enter' || event.key === ' ') {
    event.preventDefault();
    dropdownOptions[currentFocus].click();
  }
});

function hideMenu() {
  dropdownMenu.hidden = true;
  dropdownToggle.setAttribute('aria-expanded', false);
  dropdownToggle.focus();
  currentFocus = -1;
}

// Click outside to close
document.addEventListener('click', (event) => {
  if (!dropdownToggle.contains(event.target) &&
!dropdownMenu.contains(event.target)) {
    hideMenu();
  }
});
```

This JavaScript code handles:

- **Expanding/collapsing the menu:** Toggles the aria-expanded attribute and shows/hides the menu when the button is clicked.
- **Keyboard navigation:** Allows users to navigate the options using the arrow keys, Enter, and Esc.

- **Focus management:** Moves focus to the selected option and manages focus within the menu.
- **Closing the menu:** Hides the menu when the user clicks outside of the dropdown or presses the Esc key.

4. Adding Touch Support

To ensure the dropdown works well on touch devices, you can add touch event listeners:

JavaScript

```
dropdownToggle.addEventListener('touchstart', () => {
  // Toggle the menu on touchstart
  const expanded = dropdownToggle.getAttribute('aria-
expanded') === 'true';
  dropdownToggle.setAttribute('aria-expanded', !expanded);
  dropdownMenu.hidden = expanded;
});
```

5. Illustrating the Accessible Dropdown

Imagine a user navigating your website with a screen reader. When they encounter your custom dropdown, the screen reader announces that it's a combobox and that it's collapsed. The user can then use the arrow keys to navigate the options, and the screen reader will announce each option as it receives focus. When the user presses Enter, the selected option is announced, and the dropdown collapses.

This example demonstrates how ARIA attributes and keyboard navigation create an inclusive experience for users with disabilities.

CHAPTER 12: DEPLOYING AND MAINTAINING YOUR BOOTSTRAP 5 PROJECTS

12.1 Choosing a Hosting Provider

Alright, you've built your amazing website or web application with Bootstrap 5, and now it's time to share it with the world! This involves deploying your project to a web server, making it accessible to users on the internet. Think of it like launching your spaceship into orbit – you've built the vessel, and now it's time to blast off and explore the vast expanse of the web.

Choosing the right hosting provider is a crucial step in this process. It's like selecting the right launchpad for your spaceship – you need a reliable and secure platform that can handle your project's needs and ensure a smooth liftoff.

There are numerous hosting providers available, each with its own strengths, weaknesses, and pricing structures. Here's a breakdown of some key factors to consider when choosing a hosting provider:

1. Type of Hosting

- **Shared Hosting:** The most affordable option, where your website shares a server with other websites. This is suitable for small websites with low traffic.
- **VPS Hosting:** A virtual private server provides more resources and control than shared hosting, making it suitable for medium-sized websites or applications with moderate traffic.
- **Cloud Hosting:** Your website is hosted on a network of servers, offering scalability and reliability. This is suitable for websites with fluctuating traffic or high availability requirements.
- **Dedicated Hosting:** You have an entire server dedicated to your website, providing maximum performance and control. This is suitable for large websites or applications with high traffic and demanding resource needs.

2. Features

- **Storage space:** How much storage space do you need for your website's files and databases?
- **Bandwidth:** How much data transfer do you expect per month?
- **Domains and subdomains:** How many domains or subdomains do you need to host?
- **Email accounts:** Do you need email accounts associated with your domain?
- **Databases:** What type of databases do you need (e.g., MySQL, PostgreSQL)?
- **Security:** What security features are offered (e.g., SSL certificates, firewalls)?
- **Backups:** Are regular backups provided?
- **Customer support:** What type of customer support is available (e.g., phone, email, chat)?

3. Performance

- **Server location:** Choose a server location that's geographically close to your target audience to minimize latency.
- **Server speed:** Look for a hosting provider with fast servers and optimized infrastructure.
- **Uptime:** Choose a provider with a high uptime guarantee (e.g., 99.9%).
- **Scalability:** Can the hosting plan scale to accommodate future growth in traffic?

4. Pricing

- **Monthly cost:** Compare the monthly cost of different hosting plans.
- **Renewal fees:** Are there any renewal fees or price increases after the initial term?
- **Hidden fees:** Are there any hidden fees for features like backups or domain registration?

5. Control Panel

- **Ease of use:** Is the control panel user-friendly and intuitive?
- **Features:** Does the control panel provide the features you need (e.g., file management, database administration, email management)?

6. Reviews and Reputation

- **Read reviews:** Research the hosting provider's reputation and read reviews from other users.
- **Check uptime statistics:** Look for independent uptime monitoring statistics to assess the provider's reliability.

Popular Hosting Providers

Here are some popular hosting providers to consider:

- **Bluehost:** A popular choice for shared and WordPress hosting.
- **HostGator:** Offers a variety of hosting plans, including shared, VPS, and dedicated.

- **SiteGround:** Known for its performance and customer support.
- **A2 Hosting:** Offers high-performance hosting with a focus on speed and reliability.
- **DigitalOcean:** A popular choice for cloud hosting and VPS.
- **AWS:** Amazon Web Services offers a comprehensive suite of cloud hosting solutions.

Illustrating Hosting Choices

Imagine you're launching a small e-commerce website with moderate traffic expectations. A VPS hosting plan with a provider like SiteGround or A2 Hosting might be a good choice. It offers the necessary resources, performance, and security features at a reasonable price.

For a large-scale web application with high traffic and demanding resource needs, you might consider cloud hosting with AWS or dedicated hosting with a provider like DigitalOcean.

12.2 Deployment Strategies

Alright, you've chosen your hosting provider, and now it's time to deploy your Bootstrap 5 project! This involves getting your website or web application from your local development environment onto the web server, making it accessible to users around the world. Think of it like planning the journey for your spaceship – you've got the launchpad, and now you need to chart the course and choose the most efficient route to your destination.

There are various deployment strategies available, each with its own advantages, complexities, and suitability for different projects. Here's a breakdown of some common approaches:

1. Manual Deployment (FTP/SFTP)

This is the traditional approach to deployment, involving manually transferring your website's files to the web server using FTP (File Transfer Protocol) or SFTP (Secure File Transfer Protocol).

- **Process:**
  - Use an FTP client (e.g., FileZilla, Cyberduck) to connect to your web server.
  - Upload your website's files (HTML, CSS, JavaScript, images) to the appropriate directory on the server (usually the public_html or www directory).
- **Pros:** Simple and straightforward, suitable for small websites.
- **Cons:** Can be time-consuming and error-prone for larger projects, especially when frequent updates are required.

2. Git-Based Deployment

This approach leverages the power of Git, a version control system, to streamline the deployment process.

- **Process:**
  - Connect your Git repository (e.g., GitHub, GitLab, Bitbucket) to your web server.
  - Push your code changes to the repository.

    - Configure your server to automatically pull the latest changes from the repository and deploy them to your website.

- **Pros:** Efficient and reliable, allows for easy rollbacks to previous versions, suitable for projects with frequent updates.
- **Cons:** Requires some initial setup and familiarity with Git.

3. Continuous Integration/Continuous Deployment (CI/CD)

This is an automated approach that involves using a CI/CD pipeline to build, test, and deploy your code changes automatically.

- **Process:**
    - Set up a CI/CD pipeline using a platform like Jenkins, GitLab CI/CD, or GitHub Actions.

   - Configure the pipeline to build your project, run tests, and deploy the code to your web server whenever changes are pushed to the repository.

- **Pros:** Highly automated and efficient, ensures code quality through automated testing, ideal for large projects with frequent updates and a team of developers.
- **Cons:** Requires more complex setup and configuration.

4. Platform-Specific Tools

Many hosting providers offer their own deployment tools or integrations with popular platforms.

- **Examples:**
   - Netlify: Provides continuous deployment for websites and web applications from Git repositories.
   - Vercel: Offers serverless deployment for front-end frameworks like React and Vue.js.

- Heroku: A platform-as-a-service (PaaS) that provides deployment and hosting for web applications.

5. Choosing the Right Strategy

The best deployment strategy for your Bootstrap 5 project depends on several factors:

- **Project size and complexity:** Manual deployment might be sufficient for small websites, while larger projects might benefit from Git-based or CI/CD deployment.
- **Frequency of updates:** Frequent updates require a more automated approach like Git-based or CI/CD deployment.
- **Team size:** CI/CD is ideal for larger teams to ensure code quality and streamline collaboration.
- **Hosting provider:** Consider your hosting provider's capabilities and any platform-specific tools they offer.

Illustrating Deployment Strategies

Imagine you're deploying a simple landing page built with Bootstrap 5. Manual deployment via FTP might be the easiest approach.

For a web application with frequent updates and a team of developers, a CI/CD pipeline would provide automated testing, building, and deployment, ensuring code quality and efficient collaboration.

12.3 Performance Monitoring and Optimization

Alright, your Bootstrap 5 project is live on the web! But the journey doesn't end there. To ensure your website or application continues to provide a stellar user experience, you need to monitor its performance and optimize it regularly. Think of it like keeping your spaceship in top shape – you need to monitor its systems, perform regular maintenance, and make adjustments to ensure it's running smoothly and efficiently.

Performance monitoring involves tracking various metrics that indicate how well your website is performing, such as:

- **Page load time:** How long it takes for your web pages to load.
- **Time to first byte (TTFB):** How long it takes for the browser to receive the first byte of data from the server.
- **Page size:** The total size of your web page's resources (HTML, CSS, JavaScript, images).

- **HTTP requests:** The number of requests the browser makes to the server to load all the resources.
- **Error rate:** The percentage of requests that result in errors.
- **User engagement metrics:** Bounce rate, time on page, and conversion rates.

Performance optimization involves making changes to your website to improve these metrics and provide a faster and more efficient user experience.

1. Monitoring Tools

Various tools are available for monitoring your website's performance:

- **Google PageSpeed Insights:** A free tool that analyzes your web page and provides performance scores and optimization suggestions.
- **GTmetrix:** Another free tool that analyzes your web page and provides detailed performance reports.

- **WebPageTest:** A comprehensive testing tool that provides detailed performance metrics and waterfall charts.
- **Lighthouse:** An open-source tool integrated into Chrome DevTools that audits your web page for performance, accessibility, and other best practices.
- **Browser developer tools:** Most modern browsers include built-in developer tools that provide performance analysis and debugging capabilities.

2. Optimization Techniques

Here are some key optimization techniques to improve your website's performance:

- **Optimize images:** Reduce image file sizes through compression, resizing, and choosing the right format.
- **Minimize HTTP requests:** Reduce the number of requests the browser makes by combining files, using CSS sprites, and inlining small images.

- **Use a Content Delivery Network (CDN):** Distribute your website's content across multiple servers around the world to reduce latency and improve loading times for users in different locations.
- **Cache static assets:** Configure your server to cache static assets like CSS, JavaScript, and images, so the browser doesn't have to download them repeatedly.
- **Optimize your code:** Minify your HTML, CSS, and JavaScript code to reduce file sizes.
- **Use efficient JavaScript:** Avoid unnecessary DOM manipulations and use efficient JavaScript libraries and frameworks.
- **Prioritize above-the-fold content:** Load critical CSS and content first to improve the perceived loading speed.
- **Lazy load images and videos:** Delay the loading of non-critical resources until they are needed.
- **Monitor and analyze user behavior:** Track user engagement metrics to identify areas where you can

improve the user experience and optimize for conversions.

3. Continuous Monitoring and Optimization

Performance optimization is an ongoing process. Regularly monitor your website's performance, identify areas for improvement, and implement optimization techniques to ensure your website continues to provide a fast and efficient user experience.

Illustrating Performance Monitoring

Imagine using Google PageSpeed Insights to analyze your website. The tool provides a performance score and identifies areas where you can improve, such as optimizing images, reducing server response times, and eliminating render-blocking resources. You can then use these insights to implement optimization techniques and improve your website's performance.

12.4 Keeping Your Project Up-to-Date

Alright, your Bootstrap 5 project is launched and optimized! But the web development world is constantly evolving. To ensure your project remains secure, performant, and takes advantage of the latest features, you need to keep it up-to-date. Think of it like upgrading your spaceship with the latest technology – you want to benefit from improved navigation systems, more efficient engines, and the coolest gadgets.

Keeping your Bootstrap 5 project up-to-date involves:

- **Updating Bootstrap:** Regularly updating to the latest version of Bootstrap to benefit from bug fixes, performance improvements, and new features.
- **Updating dependencies:** Keeping your project's dependencies (e.g., JavaScript libraries, plugins) up-to-date to ensure compatibility and security.
- **Monitoring for vulnerabilities:** Regularly checking for security vulnerabilities in your project's dependencies and applying necessary patches or updates.

- **Refactoring code:** Refactoring your code to improve its structure, maintainability, and efficiency as your project evolves.
- **Adapting to new technologies:** Staying informed about new web development trends and technologies and incorporating them into your project when appropriate.

1. Updating Bootstrap

Bootstrap is actively maintained and regularly updated with new releases. To update your project to the latest version:

- **Check the release notes:** Review the release notes on the official Bootstrap website to understand the changes and new features in the latest version.
- **Update the Bootstrap files:** Replace your existing Bootstrap CSS and JavaScript files with the latest versions.
- **Test thoroughly:** Test your project thoroughly after updating to ensure compatibility and that everything works as expected.

2. Updating Dependencies

Your project likely relies on various JavaScript libraries and plugins. Keeping these dependencies up-to-date is crucial for security and compatibility.

- **Use a package manager:** Use a package manager like npm or yarn to manage your project's dependencies.
- **Regularly check for updates:** Use the npm outdated or yarn outdated command to check for outdated dependencies.
- **Update dependencies:** Use the npm update or yarn upgrade command to update your dependencies to the latest versions.
- **Test thoroughly:** Test your project after updating dependencies to ensure everything works correctly.

3. Monitoring for Vulnerabilities

Security vulnerabilities can arise in your project's dependencies. Regularly check for vulnerabilities and apply necessary patches or updates.

- **Use vulnerability scanning tools:** Use tools like npm audit or yarn audit to scan your project for known vulnerabilities.
- **Monitor security advisories:** Stay informed about security advisories and updates for your dependencies.
- **Update vulnerable packages:** Update any packages with known vulnerabilities to the latest patched versions.

4. Refactoring Code

As your project grows and evolves, your codebase might become less organized or efficient. Refactoring involves restructuring your code without changing its functionality to improve its maintainability, readability, and performance.

- **Regularly review your code:** Periodically review your code and identify areas that can be improved.
- **Apply refactoring techniques:** Use refactoring techniques like extracting functions, renaming variables, and removing duplicate code.
- **Test thoroughly:** Test your code after refactoring to ensure it still functions correctly.

5. Adapting to New Technologies

The web development landscape is constantly evolving. Stay informed about new trends and technologies, and consider incorporating them into your project when appropriate.

- **Follow industry blogs and publications:** Stay up-to-date with the latest web development news and trends.
- **Experiment with new technologies:** Try out new JavaScript frameworks, libraries, and tools to see how they can enhance your project.

- **Attend conferences and workshops:** Learn from experts and network with other developers to stay ahead of the curve.

Illustrating Project Maintenance

Imagine a website built with Bootstrap 4. To keep it up-to-date, you would:

- **Update to Bootstrap 5:** Replace the Bootstrap 4 files with the latest Bootstrap 5 files and make any necessary code adjustments.
- **Update jQuery:** Update the jQuery library to the latest version.
- **Check for vulnerabilities:** Use npm audit to scan for vulnerabilities in your dependencies.
- **Refactor your JavaScript code:** Improve the structure and efficiency of your JavaScript code.

This process ensures that your website remains secure, performant, and takes advantage of the latest Bootstrap 5 features.

Part IV: REAL-WORLD APPLICATIONS AND CASE STUDIES

CHAPTER 13: BOOTSTRAP 5 IN ACTION: CASE STUDIES AND EXAMPLES

13.1 Case Study 1: Building a Responsive E-commerce Website

Understanding the Project:

Let's dive into a real-world example of how Bootstrap 5 can be used to create a stunning and functional e-commerce website. Our goal is to build a responsive online store that offers a seamless shopping experience across various devices, from desktops to smartphones.

Key Features:

1. **Hero Section:** A captivating header with a large hero image, a compelling headline, and a clear call-to-action.
2. **Product Catalog:** A well-organized product catalog with filtering and search functionality.

3. **Product Details Page:** Detailed product information, high-quality images, and a shopping cart button.
4. **Shopping Cart:** A dynamic shopping cart that allows users to add, remove, and update items.
5. **Checkout Process:** A secure and user-friendly checkout process with multiple payment options.

Bootstrap 5 Components and Utilities:

- **Grid System:** Create responsive layouts for different screen sizes.
- **Cards:** Display product information in a visually appealing way.
- **Navigation bar:** Provide easy navigation through the website.
- **Buttons:** Use buttons for various actions, such as adding to cart, proceeding to checkout, etc.
- **Forms:** Create forms for user input, such as registration, login, and checkout.

- **Modals:** Use modals for pop-up content, such as product details or shopping cart summaries.
- **Utility classes:** Quickly style elements with classes like text-center, bg-primary, rounded, etc.

Code Snippet: Product Card Component

HTML

```
<div class="col-md-4">
  <div class="card">
    <img src="product-image.jpg" class="card-img-top" alt="Product
Image">
    <div class="card-body">
      <h5 class="card-title">Product Name</h5>
      <p class="card-text">Product description</p>
      <p class="card-text">$99.99</p>
      <a href="#" class="btn btn-primary">Add to Cart</a>
    </div>
  </div>
</div>
```

Design Considerations:

- **Responsive Design:** Ensure the website looks and functions well on all screen sizes.

- **User Experience:** Prioritize a seamless and intuitive user experience.
- **Clear Call-to-Actions:** Guide users towards the desired actions.
- **Fast Loading Times:** Optimize images and minimize HTTP requests.
- **Accessibility:** Make the website accessible to users with disabilities.
- **Security:** Implement robust security measures to protect user data.

Additional Tips:

- **Utilize Bootstrap's JavaScript plugins:** Leverage plugins like modals, tooltips, and carousels to enhance the user experience.
- **Customize Bootstrap's styles:** Use custom CSS to tailor the design to your brand identity.

- **Consider a CSS-in-JS solution:** Explore libraries like Styled-Components or Emotion for more flexible styling.
- **Test thoroughly:** Thoroughly test your website on different devices and browsers to ensure compatibility and optimal performance.

By following these guidelines and leveraging Bootstrap 5's powerful features, you can create a beautiful, functional, and user-friendly e-commerce website.

13.2 Case Study 2: Creating a Data-Driven Dashboard for a SaaS Product

Let's explore how Bootstrap 5 can be used to build a powerful and informative data-driven dashboard for a SaaS (Software as a Service) product. Our fictional SaaS product is "Communicate," a platform for team communication and collaboration.

Project Goal:

To create a responsive dashboard that provides users with a clear and concise overview of their team's communication activity, key performance indicators (KPIs), and actionable insights.

Key Features:

1. **Overview:** A summary of key metrics like active users, messages sent, and engagement levels.
2. **User Activity:** A visualization of user activity over time, showing trends and patterns.

3. **Communication Channels:** A breakdown of communication channels used (e.g., chat, video calls, file sharing) and their usage statistics.
4. **Team Performance:** KPIs related to team productivity, response times, and goal completion.
5. **Customizable Widgets:** Allow users to customize the dashboard by adding, removing, or rearranging widgets.

Bootstrap 5 Components and Utilities:

- **Grid System:** Create a flexible and responsive layout for the dashboard.
- **Cards:** Display individual widgets and data visualizations in an organized manner.
- **Charts:** Use Chart.js or other charting libraries to create interactive charts and graphs.
- **Tables:** Display tabular data with sorting and filtering capabilities.

- **Forms:** Create forms for user input, such as date range selection or filtering options.
- **Utility classes:** Quickly style elements with classes like text-center, p-4, bg-light, etc.

Code Snippet: User Activity Chart

JavaScript

```
// Using Chart.js
const ctx =
document.getElementById('userActivityChart').getContext('2d');
new Chart(ctx, {
  type: 'line',
  data: {
    labels: ['Jan', 'Feb', 'Mar', 'Apr', 'May', 'Jun'],
    datasets: [{
      label: 'Active Users',
      data: [120, 150, 180, 160, 200, 220],
      // ... chart options
    }]
  },
  // ... chart options
});
```

Design Considerations:

- **Clarity and Simplicity:** Prioritize clear and concise data visualization.
- **Visual Hierarchy:** Use size, color, and spacing to highlight important information.

- **Interactivity:** Allow users to interact with the data through filters, drill-downs, and customizable views.
- **Responsiveness:** Ensure the dashboard looks and functions well on all devices.
- **Accessibility:** Make the dashboard accessible to users with disabilities.
- **Performance:** Optimize for fast loading times and smooth interactions.

Additional Tips:

- **Use a consistent design language:** Maintain a cohesive look and feel throughout the dashboard.
- **Provide context and explanations:** Help users understand the data by providing clear labels, tooltips, and explanations.
- **Consider user roles and permissions:** Display relevant data based on the user's role and permissions.

- **Test with real data:** Use real data to test the dashboard's functionality and identify any potential issues.

13.3 Case Study 3: Developing a Complex Web Application with Bootstrap 5 and React

Understanding the Project:

Let's delve into a more complex project: a full-fledged web application using Bootstrap 5 and React. For this case study, we'll consider a social media platform called "ConnectMe."

Key Features:

1. **User Profile:** Customizable profiles with profile pictures, bio, and social media links.
2. **News Feed:** A personalized news feed with posts from friends and followed groups.
3. **Post Creation:** Users can create text, image, and video posts.
4. **Comments and Likes:** Users can comment on and like posts.
5. **Messaging:** Direct messaging between users.

6. **Notifications:** Real-time notifications for comments, likes, and messages.

Bootstrap 5 Components and Utilities:

- **Grid System:** Create responsive layouts for different screen sizes.
- **Cards:** Display posts, comments, and other content in a visually appealing way.
- **Forms:** Create forms for user registration, login, and post creation.
- **Modals:** Use modals for pop-up content, such as comment forms and profile details.
- **Buttons:** Use buttons for various actions, such as liking posts, commenting, and sharing.
- **Navbar:** Provide navigation options for the website.
- **Utility classes:** Quickly style elements with classes like text-center, bg-primary, rounded, etc.

React Components:

- **User Profile:** Component for displaying user information and settings.
- **News Feed:** Component for rendering posts, comments, and likes.
- **Post:** Component for displaying individual posts with interaction buttons.
- **Comment Form:** Component for creating and submitting comments.
- **Message Thread:** Component for displaying and sending messages.
- **Notification Center:** Component for displaying and managing notifications.

Code Snippet: Post Component

JavaScript

```
import React, { useState } from 'react';
import { Card, Button } from 'react-bootstrap';

const Post = ({ post }) => {
  const [isLiked, setIsLiked] = useState(false);

  const handleLikeClick = () => {
    setIsLiked(!isLiked);
    // Send like request to server
  };

  return (
    <Card>
      <Card.Body>
        <Card.Title>{post.title}</Card.Title>
        <Card.Text>{post.content}</Card.Text>
        <div>
          <Button variant="primary" onClick={handleLikeClick}>
            {isLiked ? 'Liked' : 'Like'}
          </Button>
          <Button variant="secondary">Comment</Button>
          <Button variant="secondary">Share</Button>
        </div>
      </Card.Body>
    </Card>
  );
};

export default Post;
```

Design Considerations:

- **User Experience:** Prioritize a seamless and intuitive user experience.
- **Performance Optimization:** Optimize image loading, minimize HTTP requests, and use efficient data fetching techniques.
- **Security:** Implement robust security measures to protect user data.
- **Accessibility:** Ensure the application is accessible to users with disabilities.
- **Scalability:** Design the application to handle increasing user loads and data volumes.

13.4 Exploring More Real-World Examples and Inspiration Sources

Alright, we've explored some impressive case studies of Bootstrap 5 in action. But the world of web development is brimming with inspiring examples of how this versatile framework is being used to create stunning and functional websites and applications.

Think of it like visiting a design museum filled with innovative creations and thought-provoking concepts. It's a chance to spark your imagination, learn from others, and discover new possibilities for your own Bootstrap 5 projects.

Here are some avenues to explore for real-world examples and inspiration:

1. Bootstrap Expo

The official Bootstrap Expo showcases a curated collection of websites built with Bootstrap. You'll find a diverse range of examples, from simple landing pages to complex web applications, across various industries and design styles. It's a great place to see the versatility of Bootstrap and get inspired by creative implementations.

2. Awwwards

Awwwards is a renowned website that recognizes and celebrates the talent and effort of the best web designers, developers, and agencies in the world. Many of the award-winning websites featured on Awwwards utilize Bootstrap in their design and development. Browsing through these examples can provide valuable insights into cutting-edge design trends and innovative uses of Bootstrap.

3. Dribbble and Behance

Dribbble and Behance are popular platforms where designers showcase their work, including website designs and user interfaces. Many designers use Bootstrap as a foundation for their creations, and you can find a wealth of inspiration by exploring these platforms. Look for "Bootstrap" or "UI design" in the search bar to discover relevant examples.

4. GitHub

GitHub is a vast repository of open-source code, including many projects built with Bootstrap. You can explore the code of these projects to learn how developers are using Bootstrap in real-world applications. Search for "Bootstrap 5" or specific component names to find relevant repositories.

5. ThemeForest and Creative Market

ThemeForest and Creative Market offer a wide variety of website templates and themes, many of which are built with Bootstrap. These templates can provide a starting point for your own projects or inspire you with different design approaches and layouts.

6. Blogs and Articles

Many web development blogs and publications feature articles and tutorials on using Bootstrap 5. These resources can provide valuable insights, tips, and tricks for building various types of websites and applications. Some popular blogs to follow include CSS-Tricks, Smashing Magazine, and David Walsh Blog.

7. Community Forums and Groups

Engage with the Bootstrap community on forums and online groups to learn from other developers, ask questions, and share your own experiences. The official Bootstrap Slack channel and Reddit community are great places to connect with other Bootstrap enthusiasts.

Tips for Finding Inspiration

- **Be specific:** When searching for examples, be specific about the type of website or application you're interested in (e.g., "e-commerce website with Bootstrap 5," "dashboard design with Bootstrap").
- **Analyze the code:** Don't just look at the visual design; inspect the code to understand how the website is built and how Bootstrap is being used.
- **Take notes:** Jot down ideas, techniques, or design elements that inspire you.
- **Experiment and adapt:** Don't be afraid to experiment with different approaches and adapt ideas to your own projects.

By exploring these resources and actively seeking inspiration, you can expand your knowledge of Bootstrap 5 and discover new ways to leverage its power and flexibility in your web development projects.

Part V: CONCLUSION AND NEXT STEPS

CHAPTER 14: BEYOND THE BASICS: YOUR BOOTSTRAP 5 JOURNEY

14.1 Recap of Key Concepts

Congratulations! You've journeyed through the comprehensive world of Bootstrap 5, from its foundational principles to advanced techniques and real-world applications. Now, let's take a moment to recap the key concepts you've mastered, solidifying your understanding and preparing you for continued growth as a web developer.

Think of this as reviewing your travel journal after an adventurous expedition. You'll revisit the highlights, reflect on the lessons learned, and chart your course for future explorations.

Here's a recap of the essential Bootstrap 5 concepts we've covered:

- **The Grid System:**
    - Bootstrap's powerful grid system provides a flexible and responsive foundation for building web layouts.
    - Rows and columns allow you to arrange content in a structured and adaptable manner.
    - Breakpoints enable you to create layouts that respond seamlessly to different screen sizes.
- **Components:**
    - Bootstrap offers a wide range of pre-designed components, such as buttons, navbars, forms, modals, and carousels, that streamline development and ensure consistency.
    - These components can be customized with CSS and JavaScript to match your specific design preferences.

- **Utilities:**
    - Bootstrap's utility classes provide a vast collection of single-purpose CSS classes for quickly styling elements without writing custom CSS.
    - The Utility API allows you to create your own custom utilities and extend Bootstrap's styling capabilities.
- **JavaScript Plugins:**
    - Bootstrap's JavaScript plugins add interactive functionality to components like modals, dropdowns, tooltips, and carousels.
    - You can activate these plugins with data attributes or JavaScript code.
- **Customization:**
    - Bootstrap is highly customizable with CSS and Sass.

- You can override default variables, create custom themes, and modify existing components to match your design vision.

- **Advanced Techniques:**
  - You can work with Bootstrap's source code to create custom builds, modify core styles, and develop new components.
  - JavaScript frameworks like React, Vue.js, and Angular can be integrated with Bootstrap to build complex and dynamic web applications.

- **Performance Optimization:**
  - Optimize your Bootstrap projects for performance using techniques like critical CSS, code splitting, lazy loading, and image optimization.

- **Accessibility:**
  - Bootstrap incorporates accessibility features and best practices.

    - Use ARIA attributes, semantic HTML, and keyboard navigation to create inclusive web experiences.

- **Internationalization and Localization:**
    - Design your Bootstrap projects to be easily adapted to different languages and regions.
    - Use localization libraries and tools to translate content and format data appropriately.

By mastering these key concepts, you've built a solid foundation for creating stunning and functional websites and web applications with Bootstrap 5. Now, it's time to embark on the next phase of your journey – continuous learning, experimentation, and exploration!

14.2 Embrace Continuous Learning

The world of web development is a dynamic and ever-evolving landscape. New technologies, frameworks, and best practices emerge constantly, and what's cutting-edge today might be outdated tomorrow. To thrive in this environment, it's crucial to embrace continuous learning and make it an integral part of your web development journey with Bootstrap 5.

Think of it like navigating a spaceship through uncharted territory. You need to constantly update your star charts, learn about new celestial phenomena, and adapt your course to navigate the ever-changing cosmos.

Here are some strategies to embrace continuous learning and stay ahead of the curve:

1. Stay Updated with Bootstrap

Bootstrap itself is constantly evolving, with new releases, bug fixes, and feature additions. Make it a habit to:

- **Follow the official blog:** Keep an eye on the official Bootstrap blog for announcements about new releases and updates.
- **Check the documentation:** Regularly review the Bootstrap documentation to learn about new features, changes, and best practices.
- **Join the community:** Engage with the Bootstrap community on forums, social media, and online groups to stay informed about the latest trends and discussions.

2. Explore Advanced Concepts

While this book has covered a wide range of Bootstrap 5 concepts, there's always more to learn. Delve deeper into advanced topics like:

- **Sass mastery:** Become more proficient with Sass by exploring advanced features like maps, loops, and conditional logic.

- **JavaScript frameworks:** Deepen your understanding of JavaScript frameworks like React, Vue.js, or Angular and how they integrate with Bootstrap.
- **Accessibility best practices:** Stay updated with the latest accessibility guidelines and techniques to ensure your websites are inclusive for everyone.
- **Performance optimization:** Continuously learn about new performance optimization techniques and tools to keep your websites running smoothly and efficiently.

3. Experiment and Practice

The best way to solidify your knowledge is through hands-on practice and experimentation.

- **Build personal projects:** Challenge yourself with personal projects that explore new Bootstrap features or integrate with other technologies.

- **Contribute to open-source projects:** Contribute to Bootstrap or other open-source projects to gain experience and learn from other developers.
- **Participate in coding challenges:** Engage in coding challenges and hackathons to test your skills and learn new techniques.

4. Follow Industry Trends

Stay informed about the broader web development landscape and emerging trends.

- **Read blogs and publications:** Follow web development blogs and publications like CSS-Tricks, Smashing Magazine, and A List Apart to stay updated on the latest news and trends.
- **Attend conferences and workshops:** Participate in conferences and workshops to learn from experts and network with other developers.

- **Explore new technologies:** Experiment with new JavaScript libraries, CSS frameworks, and web development tools to expand your skillset.

5. Embrace a Growth Mindset

Cultivate a growth mindset and embrace challenges as opportunities for learning and growth.

- **Don't be afraid to make mistakes:** Mistakes are an inevitable part of the learning process. Embrace them as opportunities to learn and improve.
- **Seek feedback:** Ask for feedback from other developers and be open to constructive criticism.
- **Never stop learning:** The web development landscape is constantly evolving, so make continuous learning a lifelong habit.

Illustrating Continuous Learning

Imagine a web developer who regularly checks the Bootstrap blog for new releases, experiments with new CSS techniques in their personal projects, and attends conferences to learn about emerging web technologies. This developer is embracing continuous learning and staying ahead of the curve.

Embracing the Journey

Continuous learning is not just about acquiring new skills; it's about fostering a passion for web development and a desire to constantly improve and grow. By embracing this mindset, you'll not only become a more proficient Bootstrap 5 developer but also a more versatile and adaptable web professional, ready to tackle any challenge and create innovative and engaging web experiences.

14.3 The Power of Practice

You've absorbed a wealth of knowledge about Bootstrap 5, but knowledge alone isn't enough to become a proficient web developer. It's like having a toolbox full of shiny tools – you need to actually use them to build something amazing. That's where the power of practice comes in.

Think of it like learning to play a musical instrument. You can read all the music theory books in the world, but you won't become a skilled musician until you spend hours practicing, honing your technique, and experimenting with different melodies.

Similarly, in web development, practice is essential for solidifying your understanding of concepts, developing problem-solving skills, and building real-world experience.

Here's how to harness the power of practice in your Bootstrap 5 journey:

1. Hands-on Projects

The best way to learn is by doing. Challenge yourself with hands-on projects that push your boundaries and allow you to apply your knowledge in practical scenarios.

- **Start small:** Begin with smaller projects to reinforce fundamental concepts, like building a simple landing page or a basic navigation bar.
- **Gradually increase complexity:** As you gain confidence, tackle more complex projects, like creating interactive dashboards, dynamic forms, or single-page applications.
- **Replicate real-world examples:** Try replicating websites or components you admire to learn from their design and implementation.

2. Code Challenges and Exercises

Coding challenges and exercises provide focused practice on specific concepts or techniques.

- **Online platforms:** Utilize online platforms like Codewars, HackerRank, and LeetCode to solve coding challenges and test your skills.
- **Bootstrap-specific exercises:** Seek out Bootstrap-specific exercises or tutorials that focus on specific components or features.
- **Create your own challenges:** Challenge yourself to build specific components or implement particular functionalities using Bootstrap 5.

3. Experimentation and Exploration

Don't be afraid to experiment with different approaches, try out new ideas, and explore the boundaries of Bootstrap 5.

- **Tweak existing components:** Modify Bootstrap's components to create custom variations or add unique functionalities.

- **Combine with other technologies:** Integrate Bootstrap with other JavaScript libraries, CSS frameworks, or backend technologies to expand your skillset.
- **Push the limits:** Challenge yourself to build complex and ambitious projects that push the limits of what you can achieve with Bootstrap 5.

4. Code Reviews and Feedback

Seek feedback on your code from other developers to identify areas for improvement and learn from different perspectives.

- **Online communities:** Share your code in online communities like Stack Overflow or Reddit to get feedback and suggestions.
- **Code review platforms:** Utilize code review platforms like GitHub or GitLab to collaborate with others and receive constructive criticism.
- **Mentorship:** Seek mentorship from experienced developers to gain valuable insights and guidance.

5. Consistency and Persistence

Practice consistently and persistently to make steady progress and build lasting skills.

- **Set aside dedicated time:** Allocate dedicated time for practice, even if it's just for a short period each day.
- **Break down large projects:** Divide larger projects into smaller, manageable tasks to avoid feeling overwhelmed.
- **Celebrate your achievements:** Acknowledge and celebrate your progress to stay motivated and encouraged.

Illustrating the Power of Practice

Imagine a web developer who consistently practices building different types of websites with Bootstrap 5, participates in coding challenges, and seeks feedback from other developers. This developer is actively honing their skills, gaining valuable experience, and becoming a more proficient and confident Bootstrap 5 user.

Embrace the Practice

Practice is not just about repetition; it's about actively engaging with the learning process, experimenting with new ideas, and pushing your boundaries. By embracing the power of practice, you'll transform your knowledge into tangible skills and unlock your full potential as a Bootstrap 5 developer.

14.4 Join the Community

The web development journey can sometimes feel like a solitary pursuit, but it doesn't have to be! Joining the vibrant and supportive Bootstrap 5 community can enrich your learning experience, accelerate your growth, and connect you with like-minded individuals who share your passion for building amazing things on the web.

Think of it like joining a crew of explorers venturing into uncharted territory. You can share knowledge, collaborate on challenges, celebrate discoveries, and support each other along the way.

Here's how to become an active member of the Bootstrap 5 community:

1. Online Forums and Communities

- **Official Bootstrap forum:** The official Bootstrap forum is a hub for discussions, questions, and support related to the framework. You can ask questions, share your knowledge, and connect with other Bootstrap users.

- **Stack Overflow:** Stack Overflow is a popular Q&A platform for programmers. You can find answers to common Bootstrap questions, ask for help with specific challenges, and contribute your own expertise.
- **Reddit:** The r/bootstrap subreddit is a community for discussing Bootstrap-related topics, sharing projects, and getting feedback.

2. Social Media

- **Twitter:** Follow the official Bootstrap Twitter account (@getbootstrap) and other Bootstrap enthusiasts to stay updated on the latest news, releases, and discussions. Use the hashtag #bootstrap5 to join conversations and share your own insights.
- **LinkedIn:** Connect with other Bootstrap developers on LinkedIn and join relevant groups to network and share knowledge.

3. Open Source Contributions

Contribute to the Bootstrap project itself or other open-source projects that use Bootstrap. This is a great way to give back to the community, learn from experienced developers, and improve your skills.

- **GitHub:** The Bootstrap source code is hosted on GitHub. You can contribute by reporting bugs, suggesting improvements, or submitting code patches.
- **Other open-source projects:** Many open-source projects use Bootstrap. You can contribute to these projects by helping with development, documentation, or testing.

4. Local Meetups and Events

Attend local meetups or workshops focused on Bootstrap or web development in general. This is a great way to connect with other developers in your area, learn new skills, and share your experiences.

- **Meetup.com:** Find Bootstrap or web development meetups in your area on Meetup.com.
- **Local workshops and conferences:** Attend workshops or conferences related to Bootstrap or front-end development to learn from experts and network with other professionals.

5. Online Courses and Tutorials

Many online courses and tutorials are available to help you deepen your Bootstrap knowledge and learn from experienced instructors.

- **FreeCodeCamp:** FreeCodeCamp offers a comprehensive curriculum on web development, including sections on Bootstrap.
- **Udemy and Coursera:** These platforms offer a variety of paid and free courses on Bootstrap and related technologies.
- **YouTube channels:** Many YouTube channels provide tutorials and tips on using Bootstrap 5.

Benefits of Joining the Community

Joining the Bootstrap 5 community offers numerous benefits:

- **Learning and growth:** Learn from experienced developers, get answers to your questions, and discover new techniques and best practices.
- **Support and collaboration:** Get help with challenges, collaborate on projects, and share your knowledge with others.
- **Networking:** Connect with other developers, build relationships, and expand your professional network.
- **Inspiration:** Get inspired by the work of others and discover new possibilities for your own projects.
- **Contribution:** Give back to the community by contributing to open-source projects or helping others.

Illustrating Community Engagement

Imagine a developer who actively participates in the Bootstrap forum, shares their projects on Twitter, and contributes to the

Bootstrap source code on GitHub. This developer is deeply engaged with the community, benefiting from the collective knowledge and contributing to its growth.

Embrace the Community

The Bootstrap 5 community is a welcoming and supportive space for developers of all levels. By joining this community, you'll not only enhance your learning journey but also become part of a vibrant network of passionate individuals who share your love for building amazing things on the web.

14.5 Resources for Continued Growth

Your journey with Bootstrap 5 doesn't end with this book! The web development landscape is vast and ever-evolving, and there's always more to learn, explore, and master. Think of it like reaching a scenic overlook on a hike. You've come a long way, but there are still many trails to explore and peaks to conquer.

To support your continued growth as a Bootstrap 5 developer and web professional, here's a curated collection of valuable resources:

1. Official Bootstrap Resources

- **Official Website:** The official Bootstrap website (getbootstrap.com) is your primary source for documentation, examples, and downloads.
- **Documentation:** The comprehensive documentation provides detailed explanations of Bootstrap's features, components, and utilities.

- **Blog:** The official Bootstrap blog (blog.getbootstrap.com) features announcements, tutorials, and insights from the Bootstrap team.
- **GitHub Repository:** The Bootstrap source code is hosted on GitHub (github.com/twbs/bootstrap), where you can explore the code, report issues, and contribute to the project.

2. Online Learning Platforms

- **freeCodeCamp:** freeCodeCamp (freecodecamp.org) offers a comprehensive curriculum on web development, including sections on Bootstrap and responsive design.
- **Udemy:** Udemy (udemy.com) offers a wide variety of paid and free courses on Bootstrap, front-end development, and related technologies.
- **Coursera:** Coursera (coursera.org) provides courses from top universities and organizations, including courses on web development and Bootstrap.

3. Community Forums and Groups

- **Official Bootstrap forum:** The official Bootstrap forum ([invalid URL removed]) is a great place to ask questions, share your knowledge, and connect with other Bootstrap users.
- **Stack Overflow:** Stack Overflow (stackoverflow.com) is a popular Q&A platform for programmers, where you can find answers to Bootstrap-related questions and get help with specific challenges.
- **Reddit:** The r/bootstrap subreddit ([invalid URL removed]) is a community for discussing Bootstrap, sharing projects, and getting feedback.

4. Blogs and Publications

- **CSS-Tricks:** CSS-Tricks (css-tricks.com) is a popular blog that covers a wide range of web development topics, including CSS, JavaScript, and front-end frameworks like Bootstrap.

- **Smashing Magazine:** Smashing Magazine (smashingmagazine.com) is a leading online magazine for web designers and developers, featuring articles, tutorials, and resources on various web development topics.

- **A List Apart:** A List Apart (alistapart.com) is a webzine that publishes in-depth articles on web design, development, and user experience.

5. Inspiration Sources

- **Bootstrap Expo:** The Bootstrap Expo (expo.getbootstrap.com) showcases a curated collection of websites built with Bootstrap.

- **Awwwards:** Awwwards (awwwards.com) recognizes and celebrates the best web designs and development projects, many of which utilize Bootstrap.

- **Dribbble:** Dribbble (dribbble.com) is a platform where designers showcase their work, including website designs and user interfaces built with Bootstrap.

- **Behance:** Behance (behance.net) is another platform for showcasing creative work, including web design projects that utilize Bootstrap.

6. Tools and Libraries

- **Sass:** Sass (sass-lang.com) is a powerful CSS preprocessor that enhances your styling workflow.
- **JavaScript Frameworks:** Explore JavaScript frameworks like React (reactjs.org), Vue.js (vuejs.org), and Angular (angular.io) to build dynamic and interactive web applications.
- **Chart.js:** Chart.js (chartjs.org) is a popular JavaScript library for creating interactive charts and graphs.

7. Accessibility Resources

- **WCAG:** The Web Content Accessibility Guidelines (w3.org/WAI/standards-guidelines/wcag/) provide a comprehensive set of recommendations for making web content more accessible to people with disabilities.

- **ARIA Authoring Practices Guide:** The ARIA Authoring Practices Guide (w3.org/WAI/ARIA/apg/) provides guidance on using ARIA attributes to enhance web accessibility.
- **Accessibility Testing Tools:** Use online accessibility testing tools like WAVE (wave.webaim.org) and aXe to evaluate the accessibility of your websites.

Embrace the Journey

The web development landscape is vast and ever-evolving. Embrace the journey of continuous learning, explore new technologies, and connect with the community to stay at the forefront of this exciting field.

By utilizing these resources and maintaining a curious and growth-oriented mindset, you'll continue to expand your Bootstrap 5 skills and create innovative and impactful web experiences.

14.6 Words of Encouragement

As you reach the end of this journey through the world of Bootstrap 5, remember that this is just the beginning of your exciting adventure as a web developer. You've equipped yourself with a powerful toolkit and a solid foundation, and now it's time to unleash your creativity, build amazing things, and make a positive impact on the web.

Think of it like graduating from spaceship pilot academy. You've learned the fundamentals, mastered the controls, and now it's time to take flight and explore the vast expanse of the digital universe.

Here are some words of encouragement to guide you on your continued journey:

- **Believe in yourself:** You have the potential to create incredible things. Believe in your abilities, embrace challenges, and never stop learning.
- **Embrace the creative process:** Web development is a blend of technical skill and creative expression.

Embrace the joy of building, experimenting, and bringing your ideas to life.

- **Find your passion:** Discover the areas of web development that ignite your passion, whether it's front-end design, user experience, or building complex applications.
- **Be persistent:** The path of a web developer is not always smooth. There will be challenges and setbacks along the way. Persevere through difficulties, learn from your mistakes, and never give up on your goals.
- **Stay curious:** The web is constantly evolving. Cultivate a curious mind, explore new technologies, and never stop learning.
- **Connect with others:** Join the vibrant web development community, share your knowledge, and learn from others. Collaboration and support can fuel your growth and inspire new ideas.

- **Make a difference:** Use your skills to create websites and applications that make a positive impact on the world. Whether it's building tools for education, promoting social causes, or simply creating delightful user experiences, your work can make a difference.

The web is your canvas. Bootstrap 5 is your brush. Now go forth and create!

APPENDIX A: BOOTSTRAP 5 CHEAT SHEET

This cheat sheet provides a quick reference to commonly used Bootstrap 5 classes and utilities. It's a handy tool to keep by your side as you build your web projects.

Grid System

- **Containers:**
  - .container: Fixed-width container.
  - .container-fluid: Full-width container.
- **Rows:**
  - .row: Creates a horizontal group of columns.
- **Columns:**
  - .col-{breakpoint}-{number}: Creates a column with a specified width (e.g., .col-md-6).

- .col-{breakpoint}: Creates a column with equal width across all breakpoints.

- **Offsets:**
  - .offset-{breakpoint}-{number}: Offsets a column to the right.

Typography

- **Headings:**
  - <h1> to <h6>: Headings with different sizes.
  - .display-1 to .display-6: Larger display headings.
- **Text Alignment:**
  - .text-start: Left align text.
  - .text-center: Center align text.
  - .text-end: Right align text.
- **Font Weights:**
  - .fw-bold: Bold text.

- .fw-normal: Normal weight text.
- .fw-light: Light weight text.

- **Font Styles:**
  - .fst-italic: Italic text.

Colors

- **Text Colors:**
  - .text-{color}: Applies a color to the text (e.g., .text-primary).
- **Background Colors:**
  - .bg-{color}: Applies a color to the background (e.g., .bg-light).

Spacing

- **Margins:**
  - .m-{size}: Applies margin on all sides (e.g., .m-3).

  - .mt-{size}, .mb-{size}, .ms-{size}, .me-{size}: Applies margin to specific sides (top, bottom, start, end).

- **Padding:**
  - .p-{size}: Applies padding on all sides (e.g., .p-2).
  - .pt-{size}, .pb-{size}, .ps-{size}, .pe-{size}: Applies padding to specific sides (top, bottom, start, end).

Buttons

- **Button Classes:**
  - .btn: Base class for all buttons.
  - .btn-{color}: Applies a color to the button (e.g., .btn-primary).
  - .btn-{size}: Sets the button size (e.g., .btn-sm, .btn-lg).

- **Button States:**
  - .active: Indicates an active state.
  - .disabled: Disables the button.

Forms

- **Form Controls:**
  - .form-control: Base class for form controls (input fields, select boxes, textareas).
  - .form-label: Styles labels for form controls.
- **Form Layout:**
  - .form-floating: Creates floating labels.
  - .form-check: Styles checkboxes and radio buttons.
- **Validation:**
  - .is-valid: Indicates a valid state.
  - .is-invalid: Indicates an invalid state.

Components

- **Navbar:**
  - .navbar: Base class for navigation bars.
  - .navbar-expand-{breakpoint}: Makes the navbar responsive.
  - .navbar-light, .navbar-dark: Sets the navbar color scheme.
- **Cards:**
  - .card: Base class for cards.
  - .card-header, .card-body, .card-footer: Card sections.
- **Modals:**
  - .modal: Base class for modals.
  - .modal-dialog: Container for the modal content.
  - .modal-content: The modal's content area.

APPENDIX B: TROUBLESHOOTING COMMON ISSUES

Even seasoned developers encounter hiccups along the way. This appendix provides solutions to common issues you might face while working with Bootstrap 5.

1. Responsiveness Problems

- **Issue:** Your layout doesn't adapt correctly to different screen sizes.
- **Possible Causes:**
    - Incorrect use of grid classes (e.g., wrong breakpoint prefixes).
    - Conflicting CSS rules overriding Bootstrap's styles.
    - Missing or incorrect viewport meta tag (<meta name="viewport" content="width=device-width, initial-scale=1.0">).
- **Solutions:**

- Double-check your grid classes and ensure you're using the correct breakpoint prefixes for the desired responsiveness.
- Use your browser's developer tools to inspect the CSS and identify any conflicting rules.
- Ensure the viewport meta tag is present and correctly configured in the <head> of your HTML document.

2. Component Styling Issues

- **Issue:** Bootstrap components aren't styled correctly or are missing styles.
- **Possible Causes:**
  - Incorrectly linked or missing Bootstrap CSS file.
  - CSS overrides or custom styles conflicting with Bootstrap's defaults.
  - Older versions of Bootstrap CSS cached by the browser.

- **Solutions:**
  - Verify that the Bootstrap CSS file is correctly linked in your HTML and that the path is accurate.
  - Use your browser's developer tools to inspect the CSS and identify any conflicting rules.
  - Clear your browser's cache or perform a hard refresh (Ctrl+Shift+R or Cmd+Shift+R) to ensure the latest CSS is loaded.

3. JavaScript Plugin Errors

- **Issue:** Bootstrap's JavaScript plugins aren't working correctly.
- **Possible Causes:**
  - Missing or incorrectly linked Bootstrap JavaScript file.
  - JavaScript errors preventing the plugins from initializing.

    - Conflicting JavaScript libraries or plugins.

- **Solutions:**
    - Ensure the Bootstrap JavaScript file (or the bootstrap.bundle.js file that includes all plugins) is correctly linked in your HTML and that the path is accurate.
    - Use your browser's developer tools to check the console for any JavaScript errors and debug them.
    - Check for any conflicting JavaScript libraries or plugins and ensure they are compatible with Bootstrap.

4. Customization Conflicts

- **Issue:** Your custom styles or overrides are not being applied correctly.
- **Possible Causes:**
  - Incorrect CSS specificity (your custom styles might be overridden by Bootstrap's styles).
  - Errors in your custom Sass code preventing compilation.
  - Incorrectly linked or missing custom CSS file.
- **Solutions:**
  - Review your CSS specificity and ensure your custom styles have higher specificity than the Bootstrap styles you're trying to override.
  - Check your Sass code for any errors and ensure it compiles correctly.

    - Verify that your custom CSS file is correctly linked in your HTML and that the path is accurate.

5. Accessibility Issues

- **Issue:** Your website is not accessible to users with disabilities.
- **Possible Causes:**
    - Missing or incorrect ARIA attributes.
    - Insufficient color contrast.
    - Lack of keyboard navigation support.
    - Missing alternative text for images.
- **Solutions:**
    - Review the accessibility guidelines in Chapter 10 and ensure your website meets the requirements.

- Use ARIA attributes to provide additional context and information to assistive technologies.
- Use a contrast checking tool to ensure sufficient color contrast between text and background.
- Test your website with a screen reader and keyboard navigation to identify any accessibility issues.

General Troubleshooting Tips

- **Check the documentation:** Refer to the official Bootstrap documentation for detailed information and troubleshooting tips.
- **Use your browser's developer tools:** The developer tools in modern browsers provide powerful debugging and inspection capabilities.
- **Search online forums and communities:** Search for solutions to your issue on online forums like Stack Overflow or the official Bootstrap forum.

- **Isolate the problem:** Try to isolate the specific code or component that's causing the issue.
- **Start with a fresh Bootstrap project:** Create a new Bootstrap project to test if the issue is specific to your code or a more general problem.

Printed in Dunstable, United Kingdom

71158813R00298